TEN RURAL CHURCHES

TEN RURAL CHURCHES

Edited by
John Richardson

MARC
Federation for Rural Evangelism
British Church Growth Association
Church Pastoral Aid Society

British Library Cataloguing in Publication Data

Ten rural churches.
  1. Rural churches—Great Britain
  I. Richardson, John
  274.1'082   BR759

  ISBN 0–86065–622–5 (MARC)
  ISBN 0–948704–10–1 (BCGA)

Unless otherwise noted, Scripture quotations in this publication are from the Holy Bible, New International Version, Copyright © 1973, 1978, 1984, International Bible Society. Published in Britain by Hodder and Stoughton. Used by permission.

CONTENTS

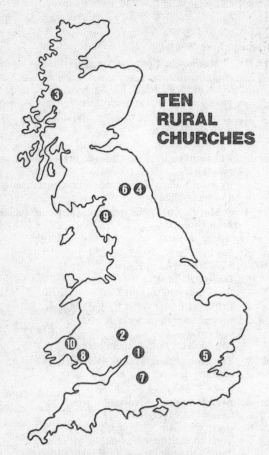

TEN RURAL CHURCHES

1 St Matthew's, Coates, Gloucestershire
2 Weobley Methodist Church, Herefordshire
3 Alvie and Insh Parish Church, Inverness-shire
4 St Mary's Abbey, Blanchland, Northumberland
5 Hedingham Baptist Fellowship, Sible Hedingham, Essex
6 Bellingham Methodist United Reformed Church, Northumberland
7 The Swanborough Team, Wiltshire
8 Bryn Moriah Pentecostal Church, Cynwyl Elfed, Dyfed
9 St Patrick's, Bampton with Mardale, Cumbria
10 Holy Trinity Church, Aberaeron, Dyfed

FOREWORD

In a world teeming with millions of needy people, why do we need a book about rural churches?

That is a good question. It could be argued that the obvious areas where Christians need to invest all their prayers and energies are the vast, shapeless urban sprawls that so often seem to squeeze humanity out of their inhabitants. Those who go in (or stay in) such areas to witness to Christ often find themselves 'weeping with those who weep' and sharing the sense of oppression that is often felt in such areas.

But there is deprivation in the countryside, also. The scenery can be pretty, but the outlook can still be bleak. With the increasing mechanisation in the farming industry, the severe curtailment of public transport and the closure of village shops, we are seeing the rise of unemployment, genuine poverty and depopulation.

At the level of caring there is much for the churches to do.

The countryside, however, is strategic. Many of the most influential people in the nation live in rural areas – at least at weekends. The late renowned philosopher and broadcaster Dr C E M Joad, after a lifetime of agnosticism, wrote a book entitled THE RECOVERY OF BELIEF. One of the key factors in that recovery was the faithful witness of rural clergy.

Rural ministry forces us to deal with real people. So often in suburban ministry where the churches are strongest, the pastor can find himself or herself totally involved with people who fit in with the accepted models of behaviour and 'style' so subtly imposed by the congregation. This is rarely the case in the country.

Again, the suburban minister can hide behind the sheer business of the task – and never get too close to the feelings and sufferings of people as they really are. This is far less possible for the country parson. As a result he or she often has a deeper and richer ministry (as well as one that brings more pain). John Berry's contribution to this book reveals something of this contrast of suburban and rural ministry.

Suburban clergy rarely luck for fellowship and resourcing. This is not always the case with many working at lonely rural ministries. I hope this book will inspire and be a good resource. It provides a way of learning and taking comfort from others.

John Richardson has long had a burden for the rural churches. He is a man totally committed to the Gospel and bursting with energy. Yet he knows that in many rural parishes things have to be 'paced' rather than rushed. To hold passion and patience in balance is a difficult thing, but if Christian ministers are to stay sane and not crack, they need to learn this balancing act. Nowhere is this more true than in rural work.

I gladly commend this book and hope that it will be read by townies and suburbanites as well as those in the country. There are lessons for all.

Finally any book that describes my own brother as a hero (p 134) has to be good!

GAVIN REID
Church Pastoral Aid Society

Introduction

Setting the Scene
John Richardson

John Richardson was brought up in a Lancashire town that accommodated both industry and a country market. He is now an ordained Anglican minister who has served in parochial ministry in Nottingham and Weymouth. Currently he is vicar of a developing new town centre parish in Nailsea, Avon. He is also Bishop's Adviser in Evangelism in the rural diocese of Bath and Wells, having previously been incumbent of four rural parishes around Dorchester, and Assistant Missioner in the diocese of Salisbury. Sue, his wife, comes from a rural background, and they have three children: Sarah, Ruth and Thomas. He is a founding member of the Federation of Rural Evangelism, Vice Chairman of the Church Pastoral Aid Society Evangelism Committee, and Resident Chaplain to the Royal Bath and West Show.

Rural England—An Eternity Away?

One Monday lunch time, three days before Christmas, I was overlooking the Tower of London from the fifth floor of the World Trade Centre. Rural England seemed an eternity away. The bustling City was throbbing with life. Decisions were being made in the offices around that would affect not only the affairs of nations, but of communities large and small. These included policies for agriculture and employment, housing and education, transport and banking subsidies, and other vital services. All this meant change for rural England.

Suddenly I was transfixed. I caught sight of a tractor pulling its trailer of hay towards Tower Bridge, followed by a lorry full of livestock, and two coaches of laughing school-children from Norfolk. In the heart of the City that lunch time the reality of rural life came home to me. Inside that 'high tech' office was a family photograph of the weekend cottage in Somerset, a holiday brochure for camping and caravan sites in Wales and Scotland, and a collage on the wall made up of various grasses. All these were pictures and images of rural England—not so far away after all.

A Variety of Models and Experiences

These ten cameos show us varied experiences of the life and encouragements of ministry in Britain's countryside today. Despite the difficulties, there is hope for the future: we forget rural England at our peril. For here in the depth of the countryside there are men, women and young people committed to Jesus Christ, who strongly believe that they must serve their Lord in the community around them. They have insecurities. They are anxious. They ask questions. How do we do it? What is involved? When will it happen? Are we good enough? Will we be trained? Can we cope? Do we know enough about our faith? Do we understand other people? What right have we to interfere in other people's lives? These are real questions that demand answers. Debate, dialogue and discussion take place in the formality of church business meetings and local parish councils. They continue informally at the school gate and over the garden fence.

A Rural Journey

From Coates in the Cotswolds to Weobley in Herefordshire we begin our journey. It takes us on in to Scotland, to Alvie and Insh, close to the resort of Aviemore. From there we travel back to North-East England, to Blanchland in County Durham; to Sible Hedingham in Essex; returning to Hexham in Northumberland before the long journey to Salisbury Plain and Swanborough. On to Wales, to Aberaeron; up to the Lake District; then back to Cynwyl Elfed before our journey ends thousands of miles later. A journey of outstanding scenic views, small communities, animals and farms, dedicated families, valleys, lowlands, rivers, grasses, trees and heathers—all can be found within Britain's colourful countryside.

In approaching the ministry of the rural church today we must ensure that what is said is not only accurate, but is portrayed in a style that does not exaggerate. This will ensure that God has the honour for what is being done among his people in the rural communities where they live and work. The smaller the community, the more encouraging the work seems to be. Congregations have reported an increase in attendance at church services of worship, with new people attending. House meetings, parish and village visitations are effective ways of helping rural church members to deepen their commitment to Christ and to each other. Planned strategies and programmes are spurs to action, and in some places evangelism is pursued enthusiastically. At the heart of community life are confident relationships between the local ministers and the decision makers. The more the laity are involved, the more lasting will be the results in church life. This rapid, ongoing change represents the ventures of faith of the participants. Flexibility and adaptability are the hallmarks needed in working together locally. Large investments of time and patience are essential as the Kingdom of God is built. For some there is no *measurable* success to point to, only the hope that God will take what is being offered and use it for his continuing witness in rural areas.

Much in the chapters will be left unsaid. The events of history yesterday bring us to where we are today—in the present. What we do now will affect the life of future generations. Yet a proper understanding of background history is crucial if we are to restore and rebuild spiritual confidence among rural Christians. *Ten Rural Churches* sets out to share something of what God is doing in the lives of communities and churches, families and individuals. This is crucial, because many village churches have not witnessed growth in living memory. Conversely, we don't want to make the accounts so 'wonderful' that leaders of other small village churches despair of their own situations. Rather, we want them to be warmed and encouraged so they will say, 'That's just like our situation: perhaps God can do it here'.

Faith in the Country

Rural life today is more complex than many people realise—according to the Proposal for an Archbishop's Commission on Rural Areas published in September 1986. It stated that all rural areas of England suffer multiple deprivation and social disadvantage which is often underestimated or denied. 'Faith in the Country' hopes to do for Christians in the countryside what *Faith in the City* did for the Christians in the Urban Priority Areas.

The report suggests that the rural community—housing, services, facilities, employment, transport, village schools, deprivation, as well as the rural church—should come under the microscope. The report has been prepared by the Bishop of Norwich, Peter Nott, and by Anthony Russell, director of the Arthur Rank Centre at the National Agricultural Centre at Stoneleigh. They examine in their proposals the background and training of the rural clergy, pastoral reorganisation, church buildings and new patterns of ministry.

About 13 million people live in Britain's rural areas, 3¾ million of whom are under the age of 14. They occupy 85 per cent of the total land area. Many of them are not contacted by any local church, especially those living on the 300,000 scattered farming communities and the 45,000 isolated hill farms.

There is hope in the countryside because rural Christians are beginning to recognise that their basic and best tools are their personal holiness and way of life. There is an openness to the challenge of the living Christ calling his disciples in the countryside to follow him by sharing a warm message of love with an often cold, scared, nervous and alienated community.

Community and Church

The Commission's proposals rightly want to examine the total rural situation and the relationship between the community and the church. Issues of economics, politics, environment, education, theology, implicit religion and tradition will need to be examined in depth. It is to be hoped that the pressure of finance and central resources will not strangle the report's hopes and expectations.

The setting up of a Commission is not likely to take place before the turn of the decade. Meanwhile, those concerned can watch and pray, wait and move forward. This is not the time for opting out of the countryside! Writers like John Poulton, Leslie Francis, Anthony Russell and John Tiller in recent years have taken up the challenge and encouraged rural Christians to move forward under God.

Ten Rural Churches offers different models, styles of leadership and situations. But all the contributors want to move forward, accepting the challenge, founding their vision upon their worship, work and witness. From their understanding of the situation they have listened to God and to each other in prayer and discussion. Over the years, strategies for different members of the local community have been worked out. Work among children, young people, families and others have all determined new schemes of pastoral care, re-ordering of buildings, re-arranging of services, reforming of structures, and the conception of specific short-term and long-term projects. At the heart of it all are different styles of personal and corporate leadership, some of which are well established, others of which are only emerging. Each is specific and flexible in its local situation.

So what of the future?

The Rural Scene

Jesus thought like a farmer. He understood the rural scene. Farming themes were at the heart of his public ministry as witnessed in his preaching, teaching and healing. He prepared his field by ploughing the furrow, digging the ground, tilling the soil, scattering the seed, fertilising the plants, harvesting the crops and burning the stubble. The example of Jesus is before us and is evident in our selected churches.

Digging the Ground

Each situation spells out the way the minister—sometimes with a small group of leaders and at other times with his Parochial Church Council or Elders or Diaconate—decides upon the ways forward. From the vision come expectation and hope. These have to be earthed in the real situation when priorities are determined according to resources available. Needs within the local communities are discerned, and over weeks and months—even years—the immediate, short-term and long-term aims and objectives are worked out. From these come strategies and programmes not aimed at survival and maintenance, but geared towards growth and new life. There is a clear sense in which prayer, Bible study, discussion, openness and the willingness to accept change are all tied up with the timely 'intervention or coincidence of God'. For example: a new family arrives in the village, or one village is given the opportunity to pastor another, or there needs to be a feasibility study of buildings and structures. All call for sensitive handling despite setbacks, clashes of personality, tradition and past histories. The way forward must be centred on shared ministry—clergy and laity working together. Gone are the days when the minister can do it all himself. Here are the days when it must be done *together*—by the whole people of God. These are signs of hope and encouragement.

Sowing

The preaching and teaching ministry of each rural church is important for its growth and development. The sermon in Sunday worship, the growth of Bible Study groups in cottages, homes and groups have all made significant contributions to the growth of rural churches. The place of relevant and lively Sunday worship, the introduction of family services, the growth of mid-week prayer and discussion groups have helped members of the regular congregation come to terms with the realities of their faith. Some congregations have learnt the dynamics of worshipping together in small groups, sometimes in their church buildings, at other times at home. But while some take up these opportunities, others see their involvement and commitment to the life of the local church in much more traditional ways.

The upkeep of the church buildings and graveyards often displays the real commitment of the local people to their village church or chapel. Much sowing time is spent in keeping a building clean and tidy. Often the people involved welcome the opportunity to speak proudly of their local situation. Such is their loyalty towards the ongoing work and witness of the local church.

Planting

With honesty and courage, *Ten Rural Churches* has described both successes and failures. There are no checklists or patterns to follow slavishly, but in each situation there is evidence of God present in power and growth, maybe in miracles, maybe in the slow developing of a life, like a flower bud opening into bloom. The local church is often the only community activity which has a place for everyone. It is an all-inclusive group. The strength of being together in worship, witness and work allows the Spirit of Christ to radiate out into the community and to permeate the quality of community life.

In the rural communities where people know each other quite well, it is often difficult for 'aggressive' and 'confrontational' evangelism to take place. Friends and neighbours can be alienated. However, oblique evangelism through friendships—building up relationships and quietly, but openly and firmly sharing personal stories and encounters with Jesus—does gradually yield results. Often in moments of crisis—either during illness, the breakdown of a marriage, problems with adolescent teenagers, or the death of a relative or friend—there are opportunities to show the love of Christ in practical 'down to earth' ways, and through the ministry of intercessory prayer.

If we are doing our job properly for Christ, then we will add much of the Spirit of Christ to the community. This means members of the local church must go out from the building and be involved in the local activities and organisations. On occasions like Christmas, Easter, Harvest and Remembrance, when many of the local residents flock into the village churches, there must be a genuine, warm welcome together with the living presence of God who attracts, stirs and challenges. Baptisms, confirmations, weddings and funerals, too, are often the occasions when peple 'turn up' to church in families and large numbers. Services connected with these family celebrations are marvellous opportunities for a clear and relevant presentation of the Good News of Jesus Christ. These occasions often provide the impetus for pastoral visiting and care over the coming months and years.

Growing

Planning for church growth means that the regular congregation has to be prepared and trained. This often means some group discussion on what it means to be a Christian, and how a living faith is worked out in humdrum everyday life. Sometimes, the life and teaching of Jesus is studied and applied to our own contemporary situation. The attractiveness of the church being together in worship Sunday by Sunday is of the utmost importance. It is the shop window to the local inhabitants. They will observe all that goes on and will only respond when the Holy Spirit quickens them to move forward. Reserve and shyness, fear and embarrassment, culture and tradition take many generations to break down. Seeds are sown, young plants break through the soil in the daylight. As they are nurtured and fed through the year, so they ripen for harvest. What is true of the seeds of nature is also true for people. Growth happens when local rural churches realise they are *open to God, because people matter for the sake of Jesus.*

There are no shortcuts to bringing new Christians to follow Jesus Christ. Time, patience, sensitivity and understanding are all crucial in winning over the new 'converts'. The sharers have to locate the seekers: that is, find who they are, where they are, and what questions they are asking. Opinion polls in the city and village following Mission England and Mission to London tell us that six out of ten people believe that Jesus is the Son of God. Therefore, as men and women seek spiritual goals and realities, there are endless opportunities for growth.

Among the precious gifts we enjoy in the country are our parish churches, often hallowed by centuries of worship. In the peace, quietness and beauty of these places locals and visitors come to find refuge from the pressures of life. As Pam Eccles says, 'I like going to our little country church because it is cool, silent and solid. I feel peaceful there. Our church is visited by a great number of holidaymakers, and when we have a visitors book that has a comment column it is very interesting to see "we found peace here".' Such awareness of the buildings we worship in is peculiar to many rural churches. For some it is the building and its atmosphere; for others it is the people and the memories.

Continued growth occurs as seekers become sharers.

They join the local church family, become more regular in attendance at worship, build on opportunities for study and the deepening of their faith. 'Locals' sometimes see the difference: they watch, wait, and then ask questions. Here opportunities are provided for more informal sharing of the Christian faith. Such encouragements provide the basis for long-term 'faith sharing' events.

Perhaps over a Mothering Sunday weekend, or at Harvest, a visiting speaker with a team of 'ordinary' Christians can be invited into the local situation. They may be invited to lead house and cottage meetings where they share their own personal experiences of faith. They will welcome discussion as the issues of life and death, faith and doubt, are painted onto a broader canvas. Schools' assemblies, uniformed organisations and mother and toddler groups provide other openings. Men can be met, either in the skittle alley of the local pub, or at a supper or breakfast in a local hostelry. Sometimes secular organisations like the Women's Institute or the Gardening Club may invite team members to take normal scheduled meetings.

From formal meetings opportunities will arise whereby meals, drinks and personal conversations are offered to the visitors. Here people can speak openly, face to face, about their more intimate feelings and desires for faith. Indeed in these situations Christianity is often 'caught before it is taught'. Hospitality, bed and breakfast, lunches and suppers, provided for a 'stranger' have often been the beginnings of a spiritual search both for those giving and receiving. In the searching ... comes the finding ... this is growth indeed.

'Faith-sharing teams' consisting of visiting evangelists, clergy and members of other churches invited by the local Christians in the community encourage conversations about the Christian faith today. The results of open debate, dialogue and discussion in homes and other informal gatherings open up the way for the more formal proclamation within the context of Sunday worship. Here the invited speaker can sum up the facts, faith and feelings involved in following Jesus as a present day disciple. He may call for

both a personal and public response. He can offer a ministry of prayer, counsel and support. Faith-sharing projects
like these have shown that God's sense of timing has been
perfect. Natural contacts have benefited as visitors have
built relationships quickly with local people.

In God's economy, no resources are wasted. The Spirit of
God blows new life and breath into local country structures,
simply because they have shared in the open hospitality of
the home. Is this the reverse of what you would expect?

When we think we know the direction our lives should go to bring
God's Kingdom to man, often we end up with things arranged to
prevent change. Wind of Spirit, wind of Change, you move at will
to rearrange our goals, our priorities, and our vision.

(Patricia Beall)

Harvesting

Sowing, growing, harvesting are natural cycles of the annual miracle of the agricultural year. They are symbolic,
too, of the natural cycle of the life of the rural church. In a
total programme of church life, there must be a blend of
worship, ministry, evangelism, social action, teaching, education and training. Where this happens there is the potential for the removal of superficiality and the possibility for a
genuine demonstration of God at work in His world. The
rural church is no exception in this way.

All our churches have examined their worship. They
have considered what it means for them to give God's love
back to himself. All believe and practise ministry to every
member of the fellowship. They are learning to accept and
to give God's love to each other. They are beginning to give
God's love to the community in their outreach. They are
building up their social action and concern among the
needy as they develop their various forms of pastoral care
within the local community.

The power and love of God are seen in crops ready to be

reaped, months after the seeds have been sown, nourished and sustained. Miracles in the spiritual sense occur where the power and love of God act in impossible situations to strengthen the believer's faith, and to encourage the ongoing life of the local church. As one teenager said at a recent church leaders' meeting, it's all to do with 'an inner warmth, and an outer glow. That is how I would describe it.' And that's exactly it: baptisms, weddings, funerals, community events and major festivals provide those opportunities for harvesting. Here we reap the sowing that goes on daily, weekly, monthly. We therefore ought to ask the late John Poulton's crucial question: 'What are we asking people to become when they consider Jesus?'

Each person in his own situation will answer differently, because no two situations are the same. All have needs of acceptance, love, wholeness, nourishment, sustenance, identity, achievement and fulfilment. We therefore need to advocate a faith founded upon a firm personal faith in Jesus Christ. This then needs to be thought through biblically, and acted upon realistically, using experiences from the past, tinged with common sense from the present. This is at the heart of apostolic Christianity where Christians in the words of the Acts of the Apostles 'devote themselves to the apostles' teaching and to the fellowship, to the breaking of bread and to prayer' (Acts 2:42). This has always been at the centre of any fellowship of believers since the Day of Pentecost. Today in the churches of rural England, the same teaching is being learnt, shared and applied, even if at times progress is slow.

Missions to villages, deanery events, festivals of faith, 'prom' praise, lay training schemes, flower festivals, preparing for Mission England—to name but a few projects—have brought many encouragements to rural communities. Indeed, working together for larger projects brings the very best out of small communities. Teamwork and the sharing of practical skills for area events motivates people for the larger cause. Local rivalry and competition, when harnessed aright, can be most productive in building up unity and harmony for the Kingdom of God.

Such events can overcome the crisis in the country, where 'a vision of heaven is the reality of the nearest shop ten miles away' (John Berry, see chapter 9). There may be public transport—well—one bus there and back on market days! Contemporary tensions in rural life mean attitudes are rapidly changing. People depend on each other more than ever before. They need to build relationships and to speak with understanding and trust. Such moves forward open up doors for 'gossiping' the Gospel.

The Next Step

Our *Ten Rural Churches* bring out the importance of prayer, patience and preparation. It is important to deal with the church and community at the point of their development in the here and now. Be aware of local traditions, the likes and dislikes. Be sensitive as you plan for personal and corporate outreach. Be prepared for failure and leave room for disappointment because a good foundation must be left for future advances and development. Use local skills at home and away. In the countryside we can never say, 'It is hopeless.' There are many signs of encouragement. The potential is great, especially when they involve ordinary people with real needs. God today is quietly, but richly, blessing the rural church with all that is necessary for its continued work. He has many ways in which he makes men, women, young people and children into Christians. There are many ways of sharing the Good News. There are many ways in which to serve, redeem and make whole the society within the countryside. God in his wisdom chooses to use ordinary people—yes country people—in using time, gifts and money.

These are days of celebration and renewal, of opportunity and of hope. We must move forward with faith and determination, overcoming frustrations and failure, difficulties and despair. God's work will continue. The doors of opportunity will continue to be open. But only if we plan for tomorrow to enlarge our vision, to increase our interest and to develop our involvement.

If the rural Christian does nothing, he casts a vote in favour of closing his church. If his horizons are purely local, he votes to stop the national and international work of God in this time of great world need. If he does his work grudgingly, he will find no joy, nor receive God's blessing. Alternatively, if he gives his resources of time, talents and monies proportionately and systematically, he will give something which will mean the local country Church can plan for the future. If he gives sacrificially he testifies to the high value he places upon Jesus Christ and His Church in ministering to every need of suffering humanity right where he is placed—in the depth of rural Britain. As he prays and considers his priorities, he will aim to seek God and to respond with joy.

It is my hope and prayer that you, the reader, will be encouraged and heartened, challenged and stimulated as you read the stories, encounters and encouragements of the work of God in *Ten Rural Churches*. So may you 'hear, read, mark, learn and inwardly digest' what the Spirit is doing in Christ's Church today.

Like Issachar, in the book of Genesis, we can see how good the countryside is. It is a resting place, and a pleasant land. We will willingly bend our shoulders to the task, and serve our master with vigour.

Chapter 1

St Matthew's Church, Coates, Gloucestershire

Andrew Bowden

'*Rich in history, church buildings, sheep, trees, money—everything except people*'

The Reverend Andrew Bowden ministers in a typically rural setting, with five churches under his wing: St Matthew's Church, Coates; St Luke's, Frampton Mansell; St Osmond, Tarlton; St Kenelm, Sapperton and St Peter's, Rodmarton. The community atmosphere and solid reliability are features which make church life in the Thames Head villages so appealing. St Luke's, once under threat of closure, is now firmly established again as an integral part of Frampton Mansell's village life.

Andrew Bowden and his wife, Sue, were both brought up in a rural atmosphere and so adapted easily to the traditions, joys and idiosyncrasies of village life in the Cotswolds. Andrew, Sue and their three daughters Polly, Hetty and Emma, live in Coates—the base for this rural ministry. In the little spare time he has, Andrew enjoys breeding rare poultry and has a keen interest in the toy theatre.

I am lord of all I survey. The 40 square miles of beautiful Cotswold countryside are rich in history, church buildings, sheep, trees and money—rich in everything except people. Scattered around this wedge of Gloucestershire south-west

of Cirencester are about 900 people in 7 separate
settlements. The largest is Coates, with a population of 300
which may rise to 500 if proposed building goes ahead.
Coates has a long main street with over 90 council and rented
houses, and a good working men's social club. Around the
edge of the village are 20 of the most desirable and most expensive executive houses in the Cotswolds. It is a tribute to
the tradition of village community life that everyone does
still do some things together! The church of St Matthew dates
back to Norman times and is just the right size for our needs.

Then there is the parish of Rodmarton—which also includes the hamlets of Culkerton, Hazleton and Tarlton.
Rodmarton (population 100) is an estate village, where
until very recently the only privately owned house was the
old rectory. The landlords are very concerned indeed about
the village and the church and go out of their way to let
houses to tenants who they believe will contribute to community life. St Peter's Church is a mediaeval yet practical
building. It is not too big and heats up very well. Culkerton
(population 60) is another village where virtually every
house is owned by the farmer landlord. It is very much a
working village with no frills, not even a village hall. The
only communal building is a little free chapel, where I vol-
unteered to take the service four times a year. (It's by far
the warmest church in the parish—except that once I burned
my cassock on the gas heater!) Hazleton (population 30) is a
large house with a dozen cottages. The owner is a Roman
Catholic, and the cottages are all let out to students at the
Royal Agricultural College. Tarlton, with its little chapel of
St Osmund, is an in-between place literally divided by the
parish boundary between Coates and Rodmarton. A good
deal of recent influx has brought the population up to 120 or
so, but it's a place where nothing 'village' has happened since
the weekly whist drive packed up in 1968.

Sapperton and Frampton Mansell (population 175 each)
were united in 1600 and have been at enmity ever since.
One was Royalist, the other Roundhead, and so it has gone
on. Sapperton is a picture-book village with the charming
higgledy-piggledy parish church of St Kenelm. It was the

centre of the Cotswold Craft movement founded by Gimson and the Barnsley Brothers, and their tradition of true community life survives. Frampton is beautiful too. But its daughter church of St Luke which was built in 1830 is purely functional inside, and the council estate, set laager-like on the crest of the hill, is entirely occupied by three families and their dependants. Frampton has always been the poor relation of Sapperton—until recently when the building of half a dozen new houses brought in newcomers who 'knew not the old pharaoh'. With their leadership the village is beginning to acquire a new sense of identity.

The Challenge

The outsider would be tempted to write off these tiny no-where places as unimportant. But the best definition I know of a village is that it is a place which the inhabitants believe to be the centre of the world: and that is certainly true of our villages. It's worth looking at the world of the small village through the living-room windows of your churchwarden. It's a rather different view from the one over the top of your desk, but it's nonetheless his real world for that. Seven separate hubs of the universe then. And five church buildings—six if you count the chapel at Culkerton—which, although they are all small enough and big enough to be practical, are an awful lot of grade one monument for 900 people to maintain.

Past History

Ten years ago there was a resident rector in each of the three ecclesiastical parishes. One died, one moved, and the Rector of Coates was forced to take on the lot. As one local put it: 'We didn't want him and he didn't want us.' Today it's perhaps difficult to realise what an appalling thing had happened. Two rectories had been sold with no financial compensation to the parishes. Moreover the resident rectors had been the lynchpins of community life for 150 years. They

had built the schools and the village halls; they had acted as
social welfare officers and youth leaders; and they usually
automatically chaired the parish council as well as the PCC.
Suddenly this full-time honorary village jack-of-all-trades
was gone. It seemed inconceivable that the villages—let
alone the village churches—could survive such a blow. The
fact that in our case they did so is in great part due to the
work of my predecessor, Tom Davison, ably supported by a
retired priest, James Turner. In two stormy years he established a workable pattern of services, abolished matins in
favour of Parish Communion, and converted from the
Book of Common Prayer to Rite B. He visited virtually
everyone leaving me an excellent card index, and he spread
the word around that *things had now changed*! But no one
can live with that sort of hatchet job for long, and after two
years he moved to another benefice, leaving the parishes to
lick their wounds and choose a new rector.

My wife and I came down one July day in 1978 to be inter-
viewed by the churchwardens and PCCs. It was a terrifying
experience. We were passed from one set of Cotswold
grandees to another, ending up with a very sticky cross-
examination by the Earl and the Admiral at Sapperton. But
fortunately my wife, who is more or less a local girl, discovered a number of mutual acquaintances in the parishes, and
also realised that she had once taught the children of one of
the churchwardens.

As a result of all this they decided that we would do, and
that since they had got a rector they could agree on, they
had better bury their differences and try to make him and
his family happy. So when we arrived in 1979, most of the
hard work was done, provided I played my cards wisely.

My Policy Assumptions

Ground Rules for Village Ministry

As I asked myself how these churches were to grow, I was
reminded of the rustic who when asked the way replied—

'Wull if I wer gwan ther, I wudn be startin from yere.'

And yet these were people for whom Christ had died, and with whom he was still involved. I could not abandon them and escape into the unreality of hothouse congregationalism. I must stand beside them and understand their bewilderment. I must seek to bring stability to an impossible situation so that what seemed 'a pig's innards' could be not only workable, but creative. My pastoral policy was taught me by my mother, herself the daughter of a rural priest: 'Give them two years to get to know and trust you, and then when you've got their confidence, you will be able to make changes.' So for two years I got to know and admire them. True, they weren't very joyful worshippers, but they were there Sunday by Sunday with a reliability and determination that would put many town worshippers to shame. They didn't know much about the atonement, but I perceived that in an entirely unostentatious way they imitated Christ-the-Servant in their daily lives. They weren't very good at talking about their religion, but as I went along the Communion rail I recognised that God really mattered to them.

Localism

They were of course fiercely defensive about 'their church' —and 'their pew' for that matter. But why not? 'Their church' had stood beside them through thick and thin over many years. They have come to it whether light of heart or in agony, and have knelt as many generations before them have knelt 'where prayer has been valid'. The church and graveyard are indeed the village's tap-root in history, and I have yet to discover a village that was the better for not having one.

The Tiller Report suggests that each settlement should have its local worship group, its local worship centre and its local autonomous organisation. My experience in these parishes has shown me how right Tiller is, for I have discovered that it is only when the local group feels secure from modern vicars and devious archdeacons that they will take down the barricades and begin to co-operate with 'them across the valley'.

The case of Frampton Mansell was particularly instructive. When I arrived, St Luke's was in the process of closure and was disgracefully neglected. There had been at least three public meetings to which no one had come. Then four new houses were built, which brought in newcomers who were shrewd enough to put cash value on the view from their homes down over the church. They persuaded me to take an evensong. I arrived to find a congregation of 75! After saying the office we held an impromptu public meeting, and we did a lot of hard talking. They emerged dazed (for I had called their bluff) but clear that if they wanted to keep the church open they could—provided they did all the work. Now for four hundred years, Framptonians had never *done* anything. Adept at complaint about what others had *not* done, 'doing' was not their scene. Nevertheless with the help of the newcomers, the miracle happened. There were fêtes (really good ones too), and sponsored this-and-thats. A wonderful set of postcards of the village materialised, and barbecues, and gymkhanas, and house to house carol singing, and suddenly Frampton discovered not only its God—but its own soul. I have to admit that the enthusiasm has not lasted for ever. But Frampton church has a future, with twenty or so people worshipping at the services; and best of all, Framptonians comprise two-thirds of the congregation at the weekly Eucharist at Sapperton parish church two miles away (a journey hardly ever made in the good old days!).

Village Religion

I discovered as I listened that though they used Christian language, most of the villagers were really Old Testament people, believing in the Ten Commandments, their duty to worship the Creator, and in the calling of our nation to be the people of God. The church belonged, not to the congregation, certainly not to the diocese, but to the village.

Their perception of the relationship between church worshippers and the others was interesting. The villagers described the congregation as 'good church workers'. They
were the ones who cleaned the church, organised the fêtes,
collected for the Children's Society, and kept it all going for
the rest. Not that they were different from the rest in their
status as Christians—it was just that village jobs had to be
shared out, and they did the church jobs while others ran
the WI, mowed the verges or organised the annual old
people's outing. A theological parallel would be to see them
as the Levites—the priestly caste of the village—'our flesh
and blood'—but doing a special job on our behalf.

Jesus said, 'whoever is not against us is for us'—and it has always seemed to me that to stamp on such associational religion in a village is folly. Out of the womb of the Old Testament
the New Testament is born; and I have found repeatedly that
taking time over village baptisms (there is so much natural
thanksgiving at a baptism), village weddings (quite literally
the only day in some girls' lives when their unique worth is
recognised), village funerals (when people are for once willing to be drawn on from veneration of the dead to contem-
plation of the Resurrection); time spent loving people at
these crossroads of their lives, is the best possible way of culti-
vating the seedbed of the village for the sowing of the gospel.

In all of these ways I listened and accepted and allowed the
wounds to heal; and gradually they came to accept and trust
me. Perhaps I wasn't being very prophetic, but it has always
struck me as significant that when Jesus was anointed to
prophesy the Good News, he promptly left his village and
exercised a peripatetic ministry. As I saw it, God had called
me to lead a disorganised group of bewildered yet devout
Christians from one culture to another. They would only un-
stop their ears, they would only begin to come, if they felt I
was on their side and understood their bewilderment.

Back in Business

I have spent so much time on the background history

because it shows why my fundamental objective must be to restore spiritual confidence. Re-organisation can help— but only if it follows healing and resurrection.

Karl Rahner's book *The Shape of the Church to Come* was the basis of our Lent teaching during the second year, and this wonderfully sensitive book set the framework for re-vitalisation. On the one hand we in the churches have accepted the role of servants to our villages—we are the Levites, doing the religious bit for those who are our brothers and sisters, members of our family. But we do this, not because 'we've been landed with it and there's no one else to do it', but because God has called us, has chosen us to be his workers in this little patch—and it is a high and glori-ous calling. He has chosen us, not because we are especially good or clever (and so it's not for us to carp and criticise), but *He* has chosen *us*! The tower pointing to the sky, the collar turned backwards, the faithful few getting out of bed on a cold Sunday morning to go to a church service which cer-tainly won't be fun—by our devotion to the duty of worship rather than by words spoken, He calls us to keep alive the rumour of God. It is this vision, gradually accepted, that has substituted cheerful acceptance for querulous complaint.

Church Services for the Regulars

No one can tell you how to run a good service in a small vil-lage church. Most advice about worship begins: 'first get a congregation of 30 together and then you can start'. But with a population of 200, that's just what you won't have on an ordinary Sunday. Somehow we had to make sense of a regular 10–20 worshippers. The root of the problem is again one of confidence. Ten is either twice 5 or half 20. Most village worship never gets off the ground because everyone spends the time wondering why X and Y and Z aren't there and getting irritated about it.

The trouble is that we are so haunted by memories of splendid services long ago, or jazzy rave-ups in suburban tabernacles, that we can't see what's obvious. After lengthy argument about Anglican chants, canticles, inaudible choirs and incapable organists, we have discovered that Coverdale's psalms *said* actually sing with the music of the spheres. We have discovered that the Communion hymn which is thoroughly embarrassing when sung by a choir of two, is a wonderful preparation if sung by all of us after the 'Our Father'. We have discovered that the dreariest part of the service, the notices, can be great fun if everyone joins in and gives out his own announcements. We have discovered to our surprise that people don't come to our village churches to admire our solemn dignity—but to relax in the homely atmosphere and even perhaps to have a little giggle when something goes wrong. (The day of our Church Overseas Service when Vanessa's coolie hat caught fire, no one complained that it was boring!) We have discovered that with so few children coming to church we can take a personal interest in them, even lionise them, and that they respond to our affection. We have discovered that because there are so few of us, even the most shy and untalented people can pluck up courage to read a lesson, or act as server, or take part in one of the rector's funny visual aid talks. We have discovered that because of the small numbers the rector, who isn't a great preacher, can speak with spot-on accuracy to our needs because he knows us that well. We have discovered that not every service has to take an hour, but with small numbers a good service taken with pace and swing can get you home in time to cook the Sunday joint. We have even discovered that we don't have to sit po-faced before a service, hardly daring to breath, wondering what we should be thinking about—but that we can actually turn round and smile at Sarah when she brings in her lovely baby, say good morning, and make her feel at home.

All in all we have, much to our surprise, come to enjoy services occasionally. What we had always thought of as a grim duty now has compensations. And we particularly value the once-a-fortnight coffee in church after the service (so much so that at Sapperton the churchwarden has frequently had to call 'time' to get us out of the place!) True, townees fresh from Rite 'A' find us a bit formal: but

when the problems of 'comprehensiveness' are explained
they usually accept our style of worship and grow to value
it.

For the Occasionals

So far I have been talking about our Sunday worship for
'the regulars'. But any village church has opportunities for
welcoming 'the occasionals'—at Harvest, Remembrance,
Christmas etc. 'The occasionals', we find, are a strange mixture of those who want to hear again echoes from their
youth, and those who know nothing of liturgical formality.
What we have discovered is that all of them have been con-
ditioned by television to expect 'good entertainment' (in
the best sense), and a bit of *visual* spectacle. (The British
Legion service is a case in point, with as much colour and
spectacle as a Walsingham Festival.)

The bridge between regulars and occasionals has in our
case been the children. How rarely village services are 'childworthy'; and so right from the start we decided to have a chi-
dren's service at each of the three main churches once a
month. This takes the form of a CPAS family service, or a
Rite B Communion with the first part 'doctored'. The hymns
are always chosen from the BBC book *Come and Praise*
(which is used by all three of the primary schools); the children 'do something', and the sermon is an illustrated talk. Of
course there is a danger that what is childworthy will not be
adultworthy, but the relatively good attendance of both children and adults shows that these services are valued.

Their success has also brought to light that the Parish
Communion has its limitations in a village situation. There
are free churchmen who worship with us and who do not
share our eucharistic spirituality, and there are others, less
committed, or simply not confirmed, who feel excluded by
the—as they see it—intimacy of the Communion.

Naturally we have had problems. We discovered that the
success of a family service depends on having a local worship committee who will sort out the children's presenta-

tion, remind parents that it's a family service, make sure the
right books are there, and so on. We also discovered that
9.15 am is too early for a family service. (In our rota the
Coates service is always at 9.15 am, Sapperton and Rodmarton at 10.30 am). So at Coates we dropped the 9.15 am
children's service and instead have six afternoon family services on obvious occasions such as Mothering Sunday, Harvest, All Saints and Christmas. Occasionally these expand
into major pageant services to which people come from all
over the benefice. A good example is our Holy Week 'Sta-
tions of the Cross'. We start off from the rectory with the
children all dressed up and waving palms, led by 'Jesus' on
a donkey (Shetland pony usually—in 1985 the pony be-
haved impeccably until we all shouted 'Hosannah', at
which point she bolted. That year 'Jesus' arrived on foot
…). We all crowd into the church, acting out the events of
Holy Week in different parts of the church. We end up with
hot cross buns round a fire in the churchyard. It's all terribly
disorganised, but there are always moments which are
deeply moving to adults and children alike – like a solo
'Kum-by-ya' by a child at the foot of the Cross. Certainly no
adult has ever complained to me that I was making a mock-
ery of the thing.

The Villages Working Together

Children's Work

I have said that after two years' consolidation, the icy grip
of fear about 'my church' began to melt, and the barricades
were gradually dismantled. The separate PCCs perceived
that there were things that should be done, and that it was
much better to do them together than separately. The most
obvious area of concern was children's and youth work.
Wendy began it all. She had tried to run a Baptist Sunday
school but had given up because she felt unsupported. She
wanted to try again. Six interested lay people met with the
Diocesan Children's Officer, and thanks to his wise advice,

we agreed not to be too ambitious. Once a month we meet
for an hour. The Link Club (linking the 7 settlements)
gathers between 30 and 40 children aged 4–11, to worship,
to follow an activity, and to play. It depends on a host of
helpers and an awful lot of cars. Small beer by town standards, but in a village context it was considered revolution-
ary enough to win a prize in the County Village Ventures
Competition in 1984. Certainly the value to the children in
tiny villages of meeting others in their peer group cannot be
overestimated.

Two important developments have stemmed from the
Link Club. First Jill, one of the helpers, determined to start
a 'proper' Sunday school. We had hoped it might be
peripatetic, but this proved impossible. It meets during the
10.30 am service at Sapperton in the school (two minutes
from the church), involves at least eight helpers, and
gathers in a few children from Coates and Tarlton as well.
When the children paddle up the aisle to share the Communion with us, all buzzing and bobbing, it lifts the heart on
the dreariest morning—as it must lift God's heart.

The other development has been the build-up of links between our three village schools. Two are church-aided, one
a county school with close church associations, and as with
all small villages numbers fluctuate wildly between 20 and
40, depending on the annual fertility rate! Each of the
schools is under periodic threat of closure, and this has led
us to develop the Link Club concept in the direction of Federation. The schools now swim together, play football together and share a sports day. There is an exchange of
teachers one day a week, and a further sharing in teaching
about computers. Our most recent venture was a joint
production of *Joseph and His Amazing Technicolor
Dreamcoat*, which was much appreciated all round. There
is a long way to go before anything final is established, but
few parents doubt the value of what we are doing already.

Youth work (with 11+) is of course 'impossible'. But we
do now have two church groups running two open youth
clubs in two of the villages; and the Christian motivation in
both cases is recognised. (One group is run by the Christian

Union from the local Royal Agricultural College where I am chaplain: the students wanted something practical to do, and our young people *adore* students!) But it has to be admitted that none of this as yet feeds into conventional church activity.

PCC Reorganisation

Shortly towards the end of the first two years we held a joint PCC study day on a Sunday at Kemble House. There were no startling conclusions, but we all got to know each other a little better, and agreed to have one joint PCC a year and to set up a Joint Standing Committee of PCC officers. The Joint PCC is always preceded by a Communion service, and on the first occasion this appealed so much that they suggested from the floor that we should have a joint benefice service on the 5th Sunday of the month. Mind you, they wanted it to be *Matins*—but ...!

In 1983 we were persuaded to have a stewardship campaign under the title—chosen by us—'Spring into Action'. It seemed natural that we should do it together. It was good that we wanted to do it together, and many good things came out of it: the splendid co-operation that developed within the steering committee, a number of groups which worked well, and a few who were touched by God.

But there were also a number of major problems. Many people ask me why we don't have one PCC. The deep reason is that each parish is at a different stage of spiritual development and has to be cared for in a different way. In the case of 'Spring into Action', we tried to suit everyone at once, and it didn't work. One parish did it well; another did it to please me; and the third went on strike! A particular difficulty on many village PCCs at the moment is the division between the enthusiasts and the others—(which I want to deal with in detail later). In this case the enthusiasts organised the campaign, but failed to carry the others with them. As a result there weren't enough convinced group leaders. This problem was compounded because the whole

concept of stewardship as used in our diocese sits uneasily
with village religion. Our excellent stewardship department believes that stewardship equals 'Christian commitment'. Now our Old Testament congregation understands
commitment to the church, commitment to God, and
straight financial appeal. They are unhappy with the *language* of 'Christian commitment', as it is presently used;
and their subconscious dis-ease with 'Spring into Action'
was shown by the way they mutually agreed to drop it like a
hot potato as soon as the last meeting was over: a classic
example of trying to drag people too far too fast, for which
I must take a major share of the blame.

The major PCC development since those days has been
to prepare for the day when the rector will not need to chair
all meetings. We also wanted to see whether PCC meetings
—which are in villages a sort of congregational house group
—could get round to considering something besides finance
and fabric. We have split the PCC into two sub-commit-
tees; the standing committee whose job is finance and fabric; the CIA (Creak(!) into Action) committee whose remit
is worship, teaching, youth, social events and outreach.
Notes are taken at each sub-committee and circulated to
the others on the PCC, so that PCC meetings don't have to
go through the same subjects all over again. We are amazed
at how this simple system has opened up things and gets
matters (on the CIA side) dealt with far faster than usual.
At the moment it seems to mean a lot more meetings, but
every new venture is like that to start with, and we can already glimpse the light at the end of the tunnel.

Magazine

The co-operative venture that works best and is most uni-
versally acclaimed is the magazine. It depends on the
enthusiasm and skill of one person, but she draws her support group from all the villages, and there is of course a val-
iant network of distributors. It goes free to every house in
the parish, and although it is unashamedly a church produc-

tion, it is also a village magazine with news of all village events. The director of an extremely high-powered 'Communication Centre' in one of the villages paid it the ultimate compliment when he said it was more in demand in his Centre than any other publication! It has done more to bind our benefice together than any other single enterprise.

Prayer

The quietest but in some ways most significant development has been the emergence of prayer support. A truly saintly person (most benefices have *one*!) intercedes for an hour each morning, and two or three others have joined her over the years. It is salutary for the priest, who is supposed to be the 'man of prayer', to find himself so busy that he has to rely on lay people to do the praying for him. Certainly I could not survive without being able to ring up Anne each week to let her know my requests. Another more formal parish prayer group began and ended for lack of support. Very exciting for me, we now say Matins publicly on Tuesdays at 7.00 am. Amid many things, I do still manage to say the offices on behalf of the parishes, and I discovered at one staff meeting that half a dozen or so others in the parish did so, too. So why not come together at least once a week to worship together? It's a wonderful way to start the day, and is somehow both utterly right and natural to the rhythm of our rural situation.

House Fellowship

Our problem with house fellowships hinges on the difficulty of integrating the enthusiasts with the others in villages. There are a number of people, many of whom came to Christian commitment in suburban parishes, who want and need a weekly fellowship meeting. But when we have such meetings, they spend most of the time complaining because 'the others' don't come. 'The others' feel no need for such meetings, and if they do come do so out of a sense of grim duty (which doesn't exactly help the meeting to flow). Thus our annual Lenten teaching meetings, which are part of the inherited tradition, are well attended (and incidentally we have great fellowship around the log fire at the Studio, a house in Tarlton). But any attempt to extend these out into the rest of the year founders for the reasons I have given.

Since this is such a common problem in villages it may be worth passing on a Trinitarian understanding of village ministry that we have found helpful. The basic village congregation is the church of God the Father, the Creator, who reveals himself in nature and in the Old Testament. They are the people of God, the holy nation. The enthusiasts are the New Testament church of God the Son, who see themselves as the Body of Christ, a tight-knit Christian family. Those outside the village church, not worshipping with us perhaps, but quite evidently doing the will of God in terms of neighbourly care, nature conservation or positive economic and community activity, are the church of God the Holy Spirit, at work in the world beyond our boundaries. Each church is authentic. Each church needs care and nurture. Each church needs the others. The New Testament church is only born out of the womb of the Old Testament. Both of them need to follow the lead of the Holy Spirit into the world beyond the church walls. We are in the business of *trinity*, not *tri-theism*. The more clearly we have come to recognise and respect our various insights, the more possible it has become for us to work together in harmony.

I have spent much of the last eight years defending 'the others' against 'the enthusiasts'. I have come to see that we should not think in either-or terms, but should seek the nurture of both groups. Two events have helped me to see this. First the Billy Graham visit, coupled with a mission to the Cotswolds by the Lee Abbey Community. Somehow it seems to be easier to take village people out of the village to a big evangelistic event than to bring the big event into the village and then expect them to go. Significantly, no one from our villages (that I know of) was brought to Christ for

the first time, but many renewed their commitment, and at
the first time, but many renewed their commitment, and at
least six went forward. Secondly, a recent parish visit to Lee
Abbey by 20 people from the benefice was really appreciated by all who went. For most of us, the charismatic
signs and the evangelical vocabulary flowed over our heads.
What convinced us was the patent genuineness and conviction of the young people who looked after us: and it moved
all of us many miles along the pilgrim road. The one clear
conviction that has emerged from this group about follow-
up is that our parish should provide proper weekly fellowship groups for those who want to make use of them.

Perhaps I should mention one other spiritual battle God
won for us.

Unexpected Help

When I first arrived I could not understand why the most
active parish with the most 'attractive' church was so badly
attended. For all its beauty the building was cold and when
you were caught unawares, frightening. One morning this
struck me so vividly that I plucked up courage to ring up the
diocesan exorcist. He is a man of great holiness and great
humour. He gently allayed my embarrassment and came to
see the place. He agreed that 'something needed doing'—
and with no external fuss whatever 'something was done'. It
was all so unobtrusive that I didn't even know 'when'. What
I can testify is that from that moment onwards the church
has been warm and welcoming, and the regular congregation has trebled. *Deo gratias.*

Ministry to Visitors

Evangelism in villages is as difficult as evangelism in the
family: and for the same reasons. But these days it isn't only
neighbours who walk our lanes. Spring brings the visitors,
and evangelism/ministry to visitors is something we do all

understand and are ready to undertake. In 1985 I tentatively asked if anyone would like to help prepare a joint leaflet for visitors to our parishes. I was swamped with volunteers of a very high calibre, and within three months the project was done and paid for. In essence it is a 'pilgrimage trail' leaflet around our churches, and local tourist boards are so enthusiastic that they are constantly ringing up asking for more. More important in some ways, it has led us to look again at our beloved church buildings through the eyes of visitors: non-Christian visitors. Does it really matter that our lancet windows are Early English c.1200 and our nave arches c.1350? Is it not more important for us to suggest to our visitors that they are like candles burning before the throne of God; or that our gothic arches are like praying hands? Is it not more important that there should be available in the church a book for people's prayer requests than that there should be a book for people's names and addresses? It's called 'church interpretation', and it's evangelistic common sense. What's more, it makes sense to the average village layman.

To Sum Up

For six years before I came here I lectured people on how to run a group of rural parishes. I blush crimson every time I think of it. This ministry of the multi-parish benefice is new and uncharted, challenging and different; and those who have not trodden this path *do not* understand. During these eight years we have all—that is the PCCs and I—learned many, many things.

We have learned patience. God's time is not our time. And though it would be nice and tidy for our records if all parishes grew and progressed together, that doesn't seem to be God's way of working. If we fretted about what isn't being done in our villages we would all have given up long ago. We have to do valiantly and well what God has called us to do, and wait for him to call others to do the other things. For we have learned to trust Him to call, and we have learned the significance of vocation. 'This is the famous stone that turneth all to gold ... A servant with this clause makes drudgery divine.' We have learned to value ourselves aright—as nothing less than 'King's Messengers'.

Our patience has been time and again rewarded. For we have seen a new couple move in, have a new idea, follow it through, and overnight others have appeared to support them; and change has happened where change seemed impossible.

Every now and then we have been tempted to rely on ourselves and on re-organisation. Time and again we have seen with our eyes that it is prayer which brings home the real goods. The ministry of prayer by Anne and the others is the most practical thing we do.

Wider Horizons

Of course there are yawning gaps.

I have said nothing about formal shared ministry. This is chiefly because our area is rich in non-stipendiary clergy. John lives in Frampton and has been ordained for nine years. To a remarkable degree he is strong where I am weak, and with that priceless gift of moving softly, softly, he has over the years won the respect and gratitude of all of us. Bill, who is retired, is a wonderful charismatic character who takes a splendid service, visits assiduously, and gives me total and unquestioning loyalty and support. Three such clergy for nine hundred people isn't a bad ratio: but it doesn't perhaps stimulate the emergence of formal local ministry. However, by our change in PCC structure we have already given more status to the office of churchwarden; and the convenors of groups and committees are also coming to have an enhanced 'dedication profile'. This year we have begun to take the first steps along the road to 'baptising' the visiting ministry already carried on by many lay people in our villages. Up until now it hasn't seemed right to formalise what is already begining to take shape: but I certainly hope that by 1990 we shall be producing our own local ministry.

So far as possible we run as an area of ecumenical experiment. No questions are asked of free churchmen, but we are very aware that this is a poor version of what unity could be. We have the benefit of their presence with us but we do not share with them the richness of their traditions.

Village religion keeps before our eyes the biblical insight that God is concerned about every aspect of Monday to Saturday life. Unfortunately the removal of the rector has tended to make the churches even more churchy than they were before. Many of our folk wear many hats, take part in many organisations. They need to be given the theological tools to help them to see how Sunday undergirds the rest of the week.

Perhaps most of all, we need to continue binding together the Old Testament and the New Testament churches in our villages, so that they support and respect each other, and begin to be aware of what the Holy Spirit is calling us all to do in the future.

One of the best things that came out of 'Spring into Action' was the campaign prayer which we still use regularly:

> *O Lord Jesus Christ, you lived in a village and you*
>   *understand village life.*
> *Help us to help our villages.*
> *May spring come into our homes.*
> *May the water of life spring up in our hearts.*
> *And may action spring from our new life in you; so that*
>   *spring sowing may bring autumn harvest. Amen.*

Chapter 2

Weobley Methodist Church, Herefordshire

Warren Bardsley

'*Here and there, people count*'

Weobley, on the edge of the Welsh border country, faces all the problems of rural farming communities, including the pressure of milk quotas and underemployment. Still, Warren Bardsley's description of the village's Methodist church offers hope. After years of revival, followed by decline, a small group of faithfully praying people helped bring the church back to a time of growth. God's question to Ezekiel— 'Son of man, can these bones live?'—met with a resounding 'Yes' in Weobley. And today, they continue to grow through outreach—assisting a neighbouring village chapel, and twinning with Saltley, an inner-city Birmingham church.

Warren Bardsley is the full-time circuit minister of this church, ably supported by a team of enthusiastic lay leaders, and by his wife Joan. He has two adult children, and his hobbies include listening to music, reading and watching cricket.

Weobley is situated in the picturesque countryside of North Herefordshire, and is one of the finest examples of 'black and white' villages in the country. There are a number of fine timber-framed buildings, and both the history and the attractiveness of Weobley draw a large number of visitors, particularly during the summer months. At the 1981 census, the population of the village was just over 1,000 and it has probably grown a little since then. The major period of growth was during the middle to late seventies, when a private housing estate was developed. Retired couples are moving into Weobley, but the statistics show a balanced spread across the age spectrum, with a third of the population under 25. Although situated in an agricultural area, less than 40 people depend directly on farming for a livelihood and over 200 members of the working population are employed in tertiary occupations (shops, offices etc), both in Weobley and other parts of the county. Local farmers are increasingly under pressure because of milk quotas and other restrictions. The primary and comprehensive schools have 500+ pupils on the roll, drawn from the surrounding area, as well as from Weobley itself. The village has a vigorous community life with a number of thriving clubs and organisations, many of which use the fine, modern village hall, built several years ago.

The Chapel: Background, Decline and Closure

The Methodist chapel is situated on the southern perimeter of the village and was built in 1861 as part of the Primitive Methodist movement, which was particularly strong in North Herefordshire. In 1897 a minister was stationed at Weobley and ministers were resident in the village from that time, right up to the mid-sixties. Many ministers came and went during that period, as Primitive Methodist ministers only stayed in one station for two or three years, but it was a severe blow to the local Methodist community when the minister was withdrawn from Weobley. This was perhaps the trough of a period of decline which had been going on for some considerable time, and which resulted in the closure of the chapel for a short period. The minutebook states that no services were in fact held during the winter of 1967–68. Vandalism had occurred and more than 100 window panes had been broken. It was decided by the leaders and trustees to re-open the building for worship on a fortnightly basis and to review the situation in 1969. It seemed as though Weobley was to become part of a depressingly familiar picture in the Leominster circuit, which had seen the decline and closure of other village chapels. It was a bitter pill to swallow for a church which had once been the head of a large and thriving Primitive Methodist circuit.

The question of Ezekiel: 'Son of Man, can these bones live?' might well have been asked of the situation at Weobley in the latter part of the 1960s.

A New Beginning

It is important to note that during the period of decline described above, there was a faithful group of people who had kept the flickering flame of faith alive, and their contribution to the ensuing revival cannot be over-estimated. People like the Lloyds, the Simons, the Hewitts and the Evans held the fort until reinforcements arrived. The first important factor in the resurgence of Weobley Methodist chapel was the coming of the Rev John Clarke as superintendent of the Leominster circuit. Mr Clarke was based at Leominster, and Weobley was one of 12 churches under his pastoral care. He saw the possibilities at Weobley, and under his prayerful leadership and encouragement, new things began to happen. The most significant single 'happening' was that a young Christian farmer and his wife who were resident in the village linked themselves to the Methodist church at Weobley.

Michael and Josephine Ware were Plymouth Brethren members and worshipped with their three children at Leominster, eight miles away. Because of the children, they had started to attend the Methodist Church in Leominster where there was a Sunday school. There they came into contact with John Clarke, who encouraged them to see the chapel at Weobley as the focal point of their Christian life and witness. Under the Wares' leadership an

'Adventurers' Club was formed. This was for young people and met during the week. It combined recreational activities with Christian teaching and by 1973 there were 50 young people attending from the village. At the same time, regular weekly Sunday services were being held, with occasional family services at the festivals, and a Bible-study/discussion group, began at Throne Farm, the Wares' home. Although the work was Christ-centred and chapel-based, the willingness of the Wares to open their home for a number of activities and meetings was an important contributory factor in the growth at Weobley. The Sunday congregations began to grow steadily.

Acceptance by the small group of 'locals' of the need for change—even their encouragement of it—was another important factor. This is well-illustrated by the reply given when someone asked: 'What will happen if the Adventurers Club ruin the paintwork on the chapel walls?' 'We'll just have to repaint it—every year if necessary!'

Another important development during this period was the introduction of Senior Citizens' teas and services on Sundays once every quarter. Residents from the old people's flats in the village were brought to the chapel for a tea prepared by the members, followed by an informal act of worship. Not only was this an important ministry to the elderly in the community, but it was one of the factors in establishing the caring reputation of the chapel in the village.

During the whole of its existence the chapel had been a single room—the traditional preaching-house—and this was used for everything from worship to social and recreational functions. This is one of the features of village chapels and is important to remember when making comparisons with buildings in urban situations. Steps had been taken some years before to remove the pews and replace them with chairs, giving the building a greater flexibility. But increasingly, the need was felt for additional space, to accommodate the growing work and enable new activities. In 1976 a small extension was added at the rear of the building: a meeting room with a kitchen and toilet facility. This

new extension was to prove a most valuable asset as the
work developed.

'The Timely Incursion of Key Individuals'

Although the renewal at Weobley was planned—especially
in the early stages—there was an element of spontaneity,
where one sensed the work of the Holy Spirit. Someone
close to the situation described it as 'the timely incursion of
key individuals', a striking way of saying that the right
people seemed to come along at just the right time! Certainly it is true that a major factor in the continuing growth
at Weobley was the arrival at crucial moments of people
with leadership potential. Mention has already been made
of the Wares, whose commitment, care and encouragement have been so important throughout the whole period.
Then there was the Lloyd family, who arrived at a time
when much heart-searching was in progress about the
future direction of the young people's work. Dentist James
Smith, his wife June and their family—Christians with a
nonconformist background, who were looking to worship
and witness in the place where they lived—have given so
much, especially in emphasising the evangelistic outreach
of the church in the local community, and the need for
strong support for world mission. There are others: the Rev
Bill Passman, a Methodist minster who teaches in Leominster, and who provided much needed pastoral care and
teaching of a concentrated nature at a time when that was
most important; David Hattatt from a United Reformed
Church background who is retired in Weobley and who
takes services on the circuit plan—a man with the rare gift
of getting alongside people of all ages, and who has helped
to build bridges across the generations; Evelyn Windett,
who runs a very successful 'Friendship Club' for elderly
people based on the chapel, and who is also URC. Others
have come more recently, each bringing their own distinctive contribution, while yet others have moved on. Some
are Methodists, some are not. Christians from a number of

Free Church backgrounds have made Weobley Methodist
Church their spiritual home. Although this has created its
own tensions because of differing expectations, it makes for
a rich fellowship, and a dynamic situation!

Churches Together

In the late 1970s new initiatives were taken in youth work.
Although the mid-week work continued, the need was felt
for a closer link with Sunday worship. A Seeker's group was
formed, which catered for the under 10s and met on a Sunday morning. A teenage group called 'After-Eights' met
after evening service in the chapel room, and this soon
began to grow in numbers. Later on a Crusaders' group met
on a Sunday afternoon for young people in the inter-
mediate age group. With the arrival of a new parish priest
in the early eighties, the Anglican church and the chapel
began to work together much more closely; a Council of
Churches was formed which included the Roman Catholic
church in the village, and one of the first fruits of this co-
operation was the decision to plan work with young people
together. Separate Sunday schools would continue up to the
age of 10; then youngsters from both churches would join
the Crusaders, and at 13 move to the 'After-Eight' group. It
is not unusual to see a group of 25 young people packed together in the chapel room on Sunday evenings, for their
weekly programme of Christian teaching and fellowship.

The ecumenical dimension becomes increasingly important. A joint prayer-healing group and joint services take
place, and—most important in a rural area—the annual
harvest festival is shared. Last year the evening service was
held in the Wares' barn and led by members of the Saltmine
Trust (an evangelistic agency)—an occasion for outreach as
well as harvest thanksgiving. The Council of Churches has
produced a leaflet with useful information for newcomers
to the village, as well as details of church worship and activities. This is seen as a service to the community.

What of the Future?

The past ten or fifteen years have seen great changes in the life of the church. Congregations have increased significantly, from the handful of people who struggled to keep the doors open, to an average of 40–45 each Sunday. There is an active, worshipping membership of 45 and a community roll of 100+. Although there is a feeling that the growth has 'peaked', it is not unusual to find 25 to 30 people in church for worship on a Sunday morning. In rural terms, that is a larger proportion of the resident population than you might find in many urban churches. At the monthly family services, it is sometimes difficult to find a seat; on a recent Sunday morning over 90 people crammed into the chapel, and there was an overflow into the corridor linking the main building to the extension! Participation in services is common and once a quarter the 'After-Eights' group prepares and leads the worship.

The music and singing has been greatly enhanced by the introduction of the new Methodist Hymn Book (*Hymns and Psalms*), and there is a willingness to learn and sing new hymns and tunes. Church stewards have been appointed, who share the leadership with the minister; the Church Council meets bi-monthly, and although there is a voting membership, it is open to all. Giving has increased significantly: as well as money raised for the maintenance of the property, support of missions and other charitable organisations, the church gives over £2,000 annually to the circuit for the support of the ministry and wider Methodist work at district level and nationally. And the fact that the past three ministers at Weobley have been missionaries in Africa, has helped to bring the world perspective of the church's mission very much to the fore.

All this is not to imply that there are no problems! There are a number of areas of concern. It has to be honestly admitted that most of the growth at Weobley has been 'transfer' growth, and this may have bred a certain complacency. We need to be looking at ways in which we can bring people *within the community* to Christian commitment. Of course, there are the usual problems with young people who leave the area for further education or to find work, and who rarely return, but this in itself presents a challenge: should we not be seeking meaningful commitment to Christ and his church at an earlier age? The fortnightly house fellowship has recently found a new direction after a period of uncertainty, and there is the ever-present challenge of fostering a 'family spirit' in the congregation, helping newcomers to feel they belong in the ongoing life and witness of the church.

There are three areas in particular where new growth is coming and needs to be encouraged, and where we can probably expect problems.

Building Up the Family and Twinning

Growth is seen not only in increased numbers, but in depth of relationships and a more sensitive caring for one another. There is a danger in any congregation for people to attend meetings but never truly *meet*. Growth in this area has to be planned for and worked at. Church family 'away-days' and weekends; Sunday lunches; social occasions—all are ways and means of people getting to know one another beyond the surface level. A recent development has been the formation of a link between Weobley and Saltley, an inner-city church in Birmingham with a large West Indian membership. In July a group from Saltley of adults and children spent a long weekend in the village, some sleeping in the chapel room. They spent time getting to know the local community and led the Sunday morning service at the chapel. In October a group from Weobley spent a weekend in Saltley, the highlight of which was a splendid Caribbean evening! There was much excitement on a cold November evening when a circuit group performed the musical drama, 'Crows and Methodists' (written to celebrate 200 years of world mission). A coach load of 35 Saltley folk arrived to share in the celebration, bringing much support and encouragement. One of the 'spin-offs' of what we hope will be an ongoing link has been the deepening of relationships in both fellowships among those who have shared in the exchange.

Reaching Out and Training

'The church exists by mission as a fire exists by burning' said Emil Brunner. Evangelism must always have priority, and not just for special occasions. As part of the ongoing outreach, 'special' events have their place. During the Mission England meetings at Villa Park in 1984, coach trips were organised following preparatory work in the village, and several people made decisions for Christ. The Saltmine Trust came for a weekend to visit schools and church groups, including a youth barbecue, and lead worship on Sunday. It is hoped to invite them back for a week of mission in the future. Scripture Union children's holiday weeks have been held, and all these special events have been organised by the churches working together. Recently the Methodist circuit has embarked on a long-term programme of mission using the resources of the Luton Industrial College and its extension scheme. The initial phase involves a survey of the community, to try to understand its changing nature, and the questions this is posing the church about its mission at the present time.

Serving and Prophesying

The church has a servant role in the community as follower of the Servant Christ, and has to know the context in which that mission is fulfilled. We have to listen before we can truly serve. Individual church members are already active in the work they are doing in the community.

Another hopeful sign is that Weobley has taken on a limited responsibility for a nearby chapel, which was in decline. With the support and encouragement of the circuit, two struggling village causes have amalgamated, and started a weekly morning family service. Some of the Weobley members have given help and support with this new venture—a salutary thought, when one realises that not too long ago, Weobley was in a similar position! This is evidence of maturity and growth, and shows what it means in the situation to be the body of Christ.

How does the church relate to its local situation and the wider world? The link with Saltley—a church in a materially deprived inner-city community, surrounded by Muslims—is helping us to recognise that deprivation is not simply an urban phenomenon. It is present in the countryside, albeit in different forms. The church must not accept the status quo; it exists for others, and if it is to be true to the gospel must seek to be a voice for the poor and for those who are being most deeply hurt by the economic changes taking place in the countryside. These issues will become increasingly important in the future.

At the end of an article written recently in the circuit magazine, the author quoted the words of Ezekiel chapter 37:5

This is what the Sovereign Lord says to these bones:

I will make breath enter you, and you will come to life. The renewal and growth at Weobley is primarily the work of the Spirit of God. Only the Spirit, and our openness to him, can keep us growing and moving forward.

Chapter 3

Alvie and Insh Parish Church, Inverness-shire

John Lyall

*'A wealth of good things ... dramatic
contrasts and simple beauty'*

Set in the grandeur of the Scottish Highlands, Alvie and Insh
Parish Church has a rich, colourful history and is now a
thriving centre for parishioners and the large number of
tourists who visit the area. Nearby Aviemore and the Cairngorms offer all-year-round attractions such as skiing, climb-
ing, hill-walking and water sports—or just appreciating
some of the most spectacular Scottish scenery. In addition,
the three churches in the parish—Alvie, Insh and Insh Village Church—offer a rich worship-life that cannot but attract
visitors in the area. The emphasis is on unity, brought about
by the Spirit and love of God, casting aside any potential
conflict caused by varying beliefs. The Badenoch Centre—a
Christian outdoor centre—serves as an extra ministry and
opportunity for outreach to visiting groups.

In this chapter, John Lyall, the full-time minister, draws his
congregation in, appreciating the gifts of young and old
alike. He has a wife, one daughter, three sons and two grand-
sons—and in the little time spare after his family and work,
John enjoys photography, gardening and hill-walking,
although he freely admits that work is as much a pleasurable
pursuit as his other hobbies!

Nestling in the Spey Valley, amidst the grandeur and beauty of the Scottish Highlands, the sparsely populated parish of Alvie and Insh enjoys a wealth of good things. Its history is rooted in ancient times, its geographical situation is unrivalled for dramatic contrasts and simple beauty. Add to this a spiritually alive congregation, meeting the needs of the parish and reaching out to the thousands of tourists who visit the Spey Valley every year, and your curiosity is immediately aroused.

Yesterday's Church

Although it is one parish, there are three places where worship is conducted regularly. Each is special and worth a mention. Insh Church, with a seating capacity for 140, has been the scene of Christian worship for many centuries. It is even possible that in the time of Saint Columba (c570) monks from Iona drove the Druids from the little hill where the church sits, above Loch Insh. It is believed that Saint Adamnan, a later Abbot of Iona and biographer of Saint Columba (c690), came to encourage this small Christian community. There is early (undated) masonry and a bronze bell which lead people to believe that there has been continuous worship since those early times; had worship ceased the bell would have been taken elsewhere.

Much speculation has gone into the history of this lovely church. Alas, the records were burnt in 1724, and although we find references to Insh Church in the eleventh century, there is little or no evidence of its history in medieval times. The present building is basically the one restored in 1792, incorporating an earlier building, and in the past 200 years it has had one or two facelifts. Clean and fresh, with the hallmark of simplicity, are the first impressions which most visitors get as they enter this little kirk. Peace and tranquillity quickly follow, and many stay to meditate quietly in this place which has seen so much prayer through many generations. The novelist and historian Nigel Tranter describes the

kirk, standing in its ancient graveyard amongst the Caledo-
nian pines, in these words: 'A lovelier place of worship
would be hard to find.'

Travel four miles north and you find Alvie Church
situated on a promontory of Loch Alvie. Once again the
position is strategic and views across the loch are magnifi-
cent, with heather-clad mountains in the autumn, water
lilies in the early summer, snow-covered peaks dancing in
the winter sunshine. Similar in shape and size to Insh
Church, the white-washed walls of Alvie Church catch the
eye of the passer-by (and the photographer) as its image is
reflected in the loch. There is no exact record of when this
church first came into being but it is dedicated to Saint
Drostan (c.520), founder of the great Celtic sanctuary at
Deer in Buchan. Worship here is linked, therefore, with
fourteen centuries of Christian teaching, stretching back to
those dim and distant days when men of vision chose this
place of immense beauty to inspire their worship and service to the living God. The centuries have seen countless
changes in peace and war. There are many tales of suffering, courage and brave witness.

One will suffice here. It is the story of William Gordon,
minister of Alvie Church for 57 years, including the bloody
and ruthless days of the '45 (the Jacobite Rising and Cullo-
den). A reward was offered by the English for the capture
of Cluny, Chief of the Clan Chattan, then in hiding in
Speyside. Mr Gordon was asked if he would negotiate his
surrender. This he refused to do since all fugitives from
either side had received food and shelter from his hands at
the Manse of Alvie. Called to account for his action by the
notorious Duke of Cumberland, Gordon spoke boldly,
'May it please your excellent majesty, I am exceedingly
straightened between two contrary commands both coming
from very high authority. My heavenly King's Son commands me to feed the hungry, to clothe the naked, to give
meat and drink to my enemies, and to relieve to the utmost
of my power, indiscriminately, all objects of distress that
come my way. My earthly king's son commands me to drive
the homeless wanderer from my door, to stint my bowels of

compassion against the cries of the needy. Pray, which of these commands am I to obey?' With perhaps unlooked-for clemency, Cumberland replied, 'By all means obey the commands of your heavenly King's Son.'

The building has been restored several times, notably in 1798, 1833, 1880 and more recently in 1952, when the architect was Sir Basil Spence who also designed Coventry Cathedral. During the restoration in 1880 a mass grave with 150 skeletons was uncovered below the floor of the church. These were re-buried in the churchyard where a stone bears this unusual inscription:

> *Who they were : where they lived*
> *How they died : tradition notes not.*
> *Their bones are dust : their good swords rust*
> *Their souls are with the saints, we trust.*

Like so much that surrounds Alvie Church, this multiple grave remains shrouded in mystery. Speculation suggests a battle or a plague. Whatever the cause, it seems far removed from the serenity which now surrounds this simple Highland church with its bright interior, its quaint wooden offering ladles and the granite plaque which records the names and dates of all the parish ministers since 1567.

The third building used for worship lies close to the RSPB Nature Reserve of Insh Marshes. It is called *Insh Village Church* and has none of the history associated with the other two. It was originally a cottage (late eighteenth century) but was converted into a small mission hall, serving the people of Insh for many years. In 1968 it was extensively altered and became designated as a church. It is now a charming little building, seating 36, with an impressive mosaic-type window in the shape of a Celtic cross. A portable pulpit, once the possession of Professor Henry Drummond, a renowned and much loved evangelist at the turn of the century, is one of the interesting features in the church. Today, complete with a recently installed belfry, this one-time cottage is a cherished place of worship for many.

The Place and the People

The parish is extensive, covering 180 square miles, much of it moorland and mountain. Aviemore, Scotland's winter playground, skirts the parish to the north and it stretches 12 miles south through the valley of the River Spey, embracing large areas of the Cairngorm and Monadhliath Mountains as well as innumerable glens and lochs. The residents of the parish are centred mainly in the villages of Kincraig, Insh and Lynchat and total 600. Forestry, tourism and the big estates account for most employment, although many who live in the parish have retired to the area because of its outstanding beauty and tranquillity. There has been considerable depopulation, and many houses have become holiday homes, but on the plus side a number of young couples and families have moved into the area to set up small businesses of their own or to become involved in tourism. Certainly, the problem of employment would have been critical had it not been for the great upsurge of the tourist industry in recent years. Many people in the parish work in the Aviemore Centre or in hotels, guest houses and outdoor centres in the valley. The impact of tourism has been so considerable that the residents of the parish are often greatly outnumbered by the visitors—and not just in summer, because the Spey Valley has rightly been described as 'A Place for all Seasons'. The Cairngorms are a magnet for the skier, the hill walker, the climber and the geologist; and the whole area throbs with wildlife, some of it unique to this part of the Central Highlands. Ospreys flying over Insh Church before plunging into the loch for their supper are a common summer sight, while whooper swans and geese throng the marshes in the winter—all part of the attraction for the visitors.

Today's Church

In statistical terms the church congregation is extremely

small. Membership over the past few years has ranged from 110–125. This includes some 20% who have little or no contact with the ongoing life of the church. A large number of very elderly people (the oldest regular worshipper is 92 years of age) are less active now but at one time played key roles in the life of the congregation. They are still a great source of strength and encouragement, and their confident trust in God shines out like a beacon and is valued by those who are younger. Although there has been little sign of numerical growth in recent years, there has been significant growth in the lives of individuals which has led to a number of important and exciting changes in the life of the congregation. Faith has become a thing to live by, not just something to attach to a religious performance. There has also been a new awareness of the church's task of outreach into the community and a concern for the wider mission to the whole world. To trace the reason for some of these changes it is worth looking at the way in which God seemed to lead His people.

In the Church of Scotland the spiritual oversight of a congregation is the reponsibility of the minster and elders who, together, form the Kirk Session. In Alvie and Insh Church this is made up of four women, eight men and the minister. Towards the end of 1978 they met to consider certain vital questions: 'Where are we? Where are we going? How do we get there? How do our plans fit in with the purpose of God?' It was easy to see the weaknesses and failings—the list was endless. Too few people at worship; little or no contact with children and young people; church life divorced from daily life; lifeless, or at least listless, worship; too much that was man-centred instead of Christ-centred. That Kirk Session meeting led to much heart searching and marked the beginning of a process of assessment and reassessment. There was a growing awareness that the body of Christ, the people of God, had to be built up in the faith. Hand in hand with this conviction was a new desire to take the gospel into every home and every heart in the parish.

Decisions

The first suggestions that emerged from that meeting were not expected to set the heather on fire, but there was a yearning to get something off the ground. It was felt that any suggestions should be practical, visible and attainable. In the end three decisions were made: (a) A small library of Christian books would be set up in each of the churches. Too many members had a limited understanding of the faith and a fairly parochial outlook on life. The intention of the library was to strengthen their faith, broaden their horizons and help them to discover what God was already doing in the lives of other people. The maintenance and promotion of the library are ongoing activities and involve considerable dedication. The books are attractively displayed in positions of prominence, new publications are added regularly, and book reviews help to stimulate interest. All in all this venture has become an increasingly important arm of the church's life. (b) A church magazine was to be produced, not a newsletter! Newsletters tend to be dull, church-centred and read by the dedicated few. The intention of the magazine was to present a fresh, attractive means of communicating the gospel to as many people as possible. It would be produced four times a year and would go to every home in the parish, personally delivered by one of the elders. In this way it was hoped to forge a link between the church and the community. The magazine is mainly duplicated, but now incorporates some photocopying, and has grown in importance and significance in the overall work of the parish. Many people contribute to its production with articles, poems, cartoons or other illustrations and news items. The next issue is always awaited with eager anticipation, and it has certainly fulfilled much of what it set out to do. (c) A Bible study group which had already been in existence was to be emphasised as an important part of mid-week fellowship and an opportunity of learning and growing. Numbers varied from 12–18 and as well as tackling various books of the Bible there was also time set aside for open prayer. This opportunity for spiritual nourishment met a real need in many lives and as people's faith was strengthened they began to see more clearly the church's task and the work that God was calling them to undertake as a congregation. Numbers have increased and although there is still an emphasis on Bible study and prayer, there is now a time for praise which has greatly added to the dynamic of these meetings.

Never satisfied with the point that has been reached, the Kirk Session has sought to encourage, stimulate and guide the congregation in a programme of consolidation and of reaching out into the community. This has taken many forms and is continually reviewed at Kirk Session meetings, where the thoughts and feelings of other people are also shared.

Worship

Church worship came under the microscope, and much has been done to bring meaning and relevance for all who come together Sunday by Sunday. In Scotland, preaching has always played a central role in church worship. Without taking away from this fact, Alvie and Insh began to see the need for more effective praise—not just singing. New hymn and song books have been introduced and the selection is now very varied, but it's not the introduction of the books so much as the growing desire to praise the Lord which has added a new dimension to the whole tenor of Sunday worship. Good News Bibles have been placed in the pews and are used to follow the Scripture readings and also the passage as it is expounded. This has helped many to become more familiar with the Bible for their own personal use, who would not otherwise have read it. Small printed cards have also been supplied to help people meditate and pray before the commencement of services; these are also appreciated by those who visit the churches throughout the week. Lay involvement is encouraged and there are often opportunities for elders and leaders to conduct worship. At family services children and parents play their part. There is a general wish to create a happy, relaxed, worshipful atmosphere: a place where people feel that they belong; where they can draw close to God and where the claims of the gospel come across simply but clearly. There are, of course, those who are suspicious of change or afraid of new ideas, and there is a concern not to cause unnecessary hurt or offence to those who have come from a different tradition or background. It isn't always easy, but most of the hand clapping, the drama and the visual aids have been taken in good part. The exciting thing is that more and more people sense that the worship is alive and that it is under the guidance of the Holy Spirit. Whoever is reponsible for leading the worship is assured of the prayer support of many and this greatly strengthens the feeling of unity. Those who are in the pulpit know that the people are with them and that all are one in Christ Jesus.

Outreach

What about outreach to the community? The magazine had already begun to make important in-roads and there was a new openness in many homes. It was clear that some individuals were making positive approaches to non-Christians but the Kirk Session wanted to extend some form of hospitality to the whole parish. Letters, attractively printed, were sent out to everyone over the age of 18, inviting them to share in a buffet supper. Over 300 people responded during a period of five evenings when an excellent meal was provided. The evenings were only lightly structured with plenty of opportunity for mixing and mingling; an odd game thrown in, a selection of slides and photographs to study, a local quiz to tease the curious and a brief opportunity to share something of Christ's love for all men. The fact that this was the church doing something for the parish— and not a fund-raising effort—had an immediate impact. The days that followed were a great time of bridge-building and similar 'parish evenings' have been repeated over several years, the format varying slightly from time to time.

Elders, who are designated a special area of the parish as their responsibility, are finding increasing opportunities to minister to the needs of everyone regardless of their church affiliation or lack of it. Ordinary members have also begun to have a deeper concern for friends and neighbours who are not Christians and it is thrilling to see God working through their faithful witness. With lives being changed and the church alert to its responsibility you can also expect to see opposition. There are certainly those who feel uncomfortable when the pressure of the gospel gets too close and they feel a little better if they can find an excuse to criticise or condemn. This small Christian community is learning to be vigilant and courageous.

Young Families

One area of special concern has been with young families. Sunday school teachers and the leaders of the Breakfast Club (young teens) have worked hard at making personal contact with the homes of all the children. As well as making the Sunday activities interesting and exciting for the children, they have arranged special events where parents could be invited and involved. This has included such things as Sunday lunch after the service, a family picnic after a Bible Treasure Hunt through the pine woods or a special celebration on Mothering Sunday. The number of families who are now part of the greater church family is evidence of the love and care exercised by teachers and leaders. Although a creche is provided for infants on Sunday mornings, it is not unknown for mothers to be suckling their babes in church; one young man made his first appearance at worship when he was six days old! Why not!

Finance

Money should never dominate the life of any church, otherwise the obsession with raising funds overshadows the vital

work of winning souls for Christ. Alvie and Insh have
realised the danger in this and have asked people to give
gladly and freely or not at all. The treasurer has worked
tirelessly at informing people of the needs of the church and
its mission. He never begs but seeks to encourage a
generous response from those who have discovered the
overwhelming grace and love of God. As lives have
changed and matured in the faith, there has been a marked
increase in Christian giving. Ten years ago there was a
struggle to reach £2,500 and today the figure is in the region
of £17,000. Over this period the sense of responsibility for
world mission has grown. Any surplus is gladly given away
each year to a variety of projects for the promotion of Bible
distribution, home and overseas mission, relief of poverty
and Christian education. Sums for this work have ranged
from £322 in 1978 to £3,500 in 1985. A new slant was given
to Christian stewardship in recent months when the church
received two large gifts of money totalling £65,000. It was
decided to enter into an ambitious scheme to provide four
amenity houses for the elderly. This will involve further
financial commitment for the church, but at a deeper level
it will involve tending and caring for those who will use
these facilities. Because this is a remote community, most
elderly people who are in need of special care have, at present, to leave the parish. This new project will help to meet
a real need and may well be another distinctive witness of a
caring church.

Visitors

If you were to worship in any of the churches, at almost any
time of the year, you would perhaps be impressed by the
number who are present. This could be deceiving because
almost always there are as many visitors as regular worshippers. This is a great source of encouragement to local
people who realise that their own worship is enriched by the
presence of fellow Christians from around the globe, and
from all denominations. This was highlighted once on a

most unlikely Sunday—the last day of the year. Sharing in
the worship on that occasion were a family of Baptists from
Leeds, a couple from a Pentecostal church near Edinburgh,
an elder from the United Reformed Church in the north of
England, several Anglicans, a pastor from Ghana, a divin-
ity student from Hungary—and the usual mixture of visitors from other Church of Scotland churches. There are, of
course, special holiday seasons when the crowds flock in.
Easter is an especially happy time and several hundred
gather for the sunrise service on the shores of Loch Insh
where Easter Day is greeted with praise and celebration
and everyone shares in a breakfast of fish and bread. In the
summer months extra services are provided to cope with
the crowds and an opportunity is given for mixing and
mingling as coffee is served, between services, from a caravan in the church grounds. Firm friendships have been
formed as people return year after year to find physical and
spiritual renewal in this place where a warm welcome is always given to strangers.

The Extra Dimension

An extra dimension which has been added to the life of this
rural congregation is the existence of the Badenoch Christian Centre within its bounds. This outdoor centre, opened
in 1976, was established to combine Christian teaching and
mission with the enjoyment of the countryside. Groups
from industry, schools, colleges, universities, the armed
services and churches come and stay. Skiing is top of the list
of winter sports and throughout the rest of the year there is
a wide variety of activities on the hills, on the water or in the
valley. Individuals and families also make use of this
purposebuilt, residential centre which seeks to foster a
friendly atmosphere and a clear Christian witness. Although under the control of the Department of Ministry
and Mission of the Church of Scotland, the centre has,
nevertheless, close ties with the local church. The minister
is also warden of the centre and most of the executive

committee are members of the church. A happy relationship exists between the two and while the centre benefits from the interest and support of the congregation, there are a number of spin-offs which enhance the life of the parish. The building itself is used extensively for certain church activities, such as parish evenings and family lunch gatherings, referred to earlier. The centre minibus has proved an asset for ferrying people to and from church and many guests bring their own special contribution to church worship and fellowship evenings. The centre's increasing popularity as a place of enjoyment and fulfilment is due in no small measure to the welcome visitors receive from everyone in the community.

The Power Behind the Parish

The strength of today's church rests firmly on the inheritance handed down through the faithful witness and the prayers of past generations. Long before the Kirk Session began to look more seriously at its duties, there was a nucleus of caring and concerned Christian people who were praying for the renewal of church life in this part of Scotland. Today it is obvious that the only things which have had transforming power and lasting value are those which had their roots in prayer. Perhaps the most significant change has been the breakthrough in prayer itself. It could be said that people once said their prayers but now they have started praying. The first step in this direction was a small, monthly prayer meeting made up of people from different denominations and parishes. In Alvie and Insh, it was the ladies of the Woman's Guild who took the initiative. They asked the minister for a list of all children baptised over the past five years. The reason? They had a burden on their hearts for the families in the parish and committed themselves to pray regularly for these children and their homes. A prayer card was then produced to encourage people to pray for specific aspects of the church's work on different days of the week. Prayer became a more normal and natural part of everyday life. People were beginning to have informal times of prayer with friends. Some people set aside time to meet in one of the churches for sustained prayer. Prayer vigils have become a regular occurrence when a chain of unbroken prayer is maintained in one of the churches over a period of twenty-four hours. These have usually focused on some particular area of concern such as the Toxteth and Handsworth riots. A ladies' prayer circle meets weekly. Where a crisis blows up or where there is a special cry for help, it is possible to contact a group of people who will immediately bring these issues to the throne of grace. If the Kirk Session began by wondering where they were going, it is interesting to note that they now spend far more time trying to discover where God wants his church to go.

Churches are often branded by their particular theological emphasis. In Alvie and Insh there is a rich mixture of evangelical, charismatic and traditional beliefs. This potential source of conflict is being overcome by a deeper desire to preserve the unity which the Spirit gives by means of the peace which binds the people of God together.

Chapter 4

St Mary's Abbey, Blanchland, Northumberland

John Durnford

'Speak, Lord, your servants are listening'

John Durnford has an experimental, full-time rural ministry serving four country parishes, stretching into two dioceses and two counties. He lives at Blanchland, where part of the remains of an ancient twelfth-century abbey was rebuilt to serve as the parish church. The different backgrounds of each village still affect life today: monks, railwaymen, miners and farmers have all made their own special contribution to the area. Today these parishes are trying to discover their future—whether they can act as a group without destroying their own identity. Tourism is one of the new challenges at Blanchland, as about 10,000 people each year visit Blanchland Abbey.

John Durnford has been at Blanchland since 1984, having previously ministered in Yorkshire and Zimbabwe. He was brought up in Northumberland and so feels he is 'returning to his roots'. A sense of emotional commitment therefore comes out strongly through the words of this chapter. John is married to Angela, and they have three adult children. He enjoys country pursuits and working on the large garden inherited with the Blanchland vicarage!

Bred in Northumberland and accepted for ordination through the diocese of Newcastle I have always had a desire to work in that county. 54 years after my first arrival as a babe in arms, followed by ministry in Yorkshire, 14 years in Zimbabwe, and another 8 in Yorkshire, on July 17th, 1984 I found myself back in Northumberland by 300 yards! On that day I was appointed as priest-in-charge of Blanchland and Hunstanworth in the diocese of Newcastle, and the next day I was welcomed at Edmundbyers as priest-in-charge of Edmundbyers and Muggleswick in the diocese of Durham. I am sure that God must have a sense of humour! I soon discovered my responsibilities: 4 parishes with a total population of under 500 people, 5 places of worship, 4 church councils, 2 clergy chapters, 2 deanery synods, 2 bishops, care of the thousands of visitors who come to Blanchland each year, family responsibilities, and a large garden.

The Past

Where are these faraway places with strange-sounding names, and what is their background? Blanchland is a remote village 25 miles south-west of Newcastle and 10 miles south of Hexham, at the edge of the moors of the Northern Pennines. The village is built round a restored Abbey, now used as a parish church, and the name of 'Blanchland' is probably derived from the white canons of the Premonstratensian Order (founded by Norbert in the twelfth century and originating from Premontre in France). They arrived in Blanchland about 1165, and the village gradually developed under their care; they were involved in agriculture and lead mining, and even found time to hunt the local game and create fish-ponds. The Abbey became a ruin after the dissolution of the monasteries, and the village was neglected. In 1699 a bishop's romance was to alter the future of the village, when Lord Crewe, Bishop of Durham, married Dorothy Forster who had a share in both Blanchland and Bamburgh, further north on the coast of Northumberland. After the bishop's death, estates in these villages were handed to the Lord Crewe Trustees, and under their care Blanchland was gradually restored, part of the Abbey was rebuilt as a parish church, and a resident vicar was appointed.

Today the whole village and some neighbouring farms still belong to the Lord Crewe Trustees, and nearly all of the 132 inhabitants are their tenants. The Lord Crewe Arms, formerly the Abbot's house and then a private dwelling, is now a well-known hotel, and tourists come to Blanchland throughout the year.

Higher up the valley is the little hamlet of Hunstanworth, only two miles distant from Blanchland, yet with its own distinctive atmosphere. Originally an area of hill farming and hunting, Hunstanworth was developed by a squire parson, the Rev David Capper, Rector of Huntley in Gloucestershire. He built a large house at Newbiggin, and in 1862 employed an architect of French origin, J H Teulon, to rebuild the parish church and the neighbouring houses in the Burgundian style of architecture. Next to Hunstanworth is the deserted hamlet of Ramshaw, which was in the past part of a considerable complex of lead mines in the area. The land is riddled with the remains of former workings, for which water-power was provided by a local stream, and a smelter constructed.

Four miles away from Blanchland and in a different county is the village of Edmundbyers, originally a rather isolated community, as shown by the court records of the fourteenth century. Problems about grazing lands and disputes about boundaries were very common, as was discussion about the removal of 'gold'—probably ragwort. Today Edmundbyers is surrounded by moors and farmland. Some farmers live in the village, which is a mixture of old and new. Scattered amongst the old houses are several new buildings which belong either to retired people or professional commuters, including several teachers, a chemist, a solicitor, and a local surgeon who purchased the former vicarage. Edmundbyers is the only place in the area where there is limited building, but plots and houses are expensive, making it very difficult for local people, and especially young couples, to own their homes.

Just over the hill from Edmundbyers is the scattered hamlet of Muggleswick, consisting of farms and a few private houses. The Manor of Muggleswick, originally in the hands of the Bishop of Durham, was later granted to the Prior of the convent of Durham. Sections of the grange built in 1272 are still standing. These served partly as a permanent residence, partly as a hunting lodge, and partly as a storehouse for both animals and goods. Today the area of the parish of Muggleswick is one of the largest in the diocese of Durham; yet the total population, which includes the area of Waskerley, is about 75 people. Railway enthusiasts will be interested in the background of this former railway village, where there used to be a railway line over the moors, but when the line was closed, the village began to die. In 1956 Waskerley was almost totally destroyed, leaving only the chapel (now a barn), the post office (where the former postmistress still lives), one farm, and the little church of St Matthew's where services are held once a month in summer.

Past and Present

What do we discover, when we look at our four parishes? How much does the past still affect the present? What characteristics do our parishes share in common? How are they different? All four are small and independent communities, with a great deal of local pride. Although quarrels can sometimes affect family relationships for generations, people are generally kind to each other. The past has seen a great variety of people—monks, farmers, miners, railwaymen and travellers. Today there is still a wide variety of people in the area, especially as the journey to Newcastle or Durham takes less than an hour. All share some of the effects of rural deprivation. There are no longer any schools in the area of our four parishes, communications are limited with four buses each way to Consett on weekdays, and medical facilities are limited.

Yet in other respects these small communities are not similar; they have a different feeling about them, even though the populations are so small. One of the reasons is that in the past there were local tensions between Blanchland and Hunstanworth, between farmers and miners, and at Muggleswick tensions between the farmers and the railwaymen. Housing is one of the keys to the local situation. Owing to the special relationship with the Lord Crewe Estates, Blanchland tends to be a traditional and interrelated community, leaving decisions to the landlord; Edmundbyers, on the other hand, is very different: modern houses have been built in the village, professional people have been able to purchase their own homes, and there are always some changes in population.

What has been happening to the churches in our area during the past 40 years? How have changes in the life of the church affected these remote parts of the countryside?

Pastoral re-organisation has been one of the urgent tasks of the church, and has affected many rural areas like ourselves. In 1929 each of the four parishes had its own residential priest, whereas in 1987 I am priest-in-charge of the whole area. Today only one chapel remains, Baybridge, between Blanchland and Hunstanworth. Closure of church schools at Hunstanworth and Blanchland removed an important contact with the children of these villages.

Parish registers need careful interpretation, especially as new patterns of worship have developed with the stress on the Parish Communion. Figures at Blanchland show little change. Average Sunday communicants in November were as follows—November 1971, 11; November 1976, 12; November 1986, 14. The confirmation lists at Blanchland and Hunstanworth record 32 people being confirmed since 1969, but only 2 of these have been males.

Financially, there has been a minor revolution. In the past, quotas were small; many country clergy had private income, and met expenses out of their pocket. In 1986, the combined annual quota of the 4 parishes was £3,400, and annual expenses of office about £1,500, making a total of nearly £5,000 for an area with a population of less than 500. Thankfully we are able to meet all expenses, with the help of the tourist income at Blanchland, income from the sale of property at Hunstanworth and the assistance of Manpower Services, who have been a wonderful help with schemes for church buildings and churchyards.

Difficulties abound. On the most part, congregations consist of many more women than men, and the average age is growing. All the same, I am still humbled by the good will of almost everyone in the area towards the church. Apathy exists in many of the homes, but very rarely do we meet any hostility.

Facts are not enough, nor are they easy to find. Feelings, too, about places and people are so important, and it is vital for clergy to try and understand the popular feelings about religion, and to realise the great differences between urban and rural ministry. In a town parish of any size the majority of one's ministry is with those who have some connection with the church, but in the country the local vicar is part and parcel of the whole community. In some towns, many do not even know the location of their parish church, let alone the name of their vicar, but in the countryside the local church is part of the landscape. All feel that they belong, whether they worship or not, especially those who have connections through baptisms or marriages or funerals.

Both the cycle of the church's year and that of the family provide many opportunities in a country parish. Last Christmas over 120 people attended the carol service at Blanchland Abbey; even allowing for the fact that there was a bus-load of 30 visitors, about 45% of the population of Blanchland and Hunstanworth worshipped over Christmas. If that had happened at my last parish of Hebden Bridge, with a population of 6,000, we would have had to arrange a series of carol services. Another difference can be seen at funerals; several places in Yorkshire now possess chapels of rest, where more funeral services are taken than at parish churches, whereas it is a very rare occasion in the countryside when people are not buried at the local church.

Feelings, too, about clergy can affect relationships for good or bad. A timely visit to the local hospital, or a carefully prepared service at a marriage or funeral will be remembered for many years; the opposite, of course, is still true. An impatient remark or a rushed service can harden attitudes for months. Harm is sometimes caused by trying to apply urban standards to a country situation. Nor is the countryside a rest cure, especially as more clergy are serving multi-parish appointments; in the past many clergy have been sent to the country to serve their final years before retirement. Others have found themselves in the countryside with little or no preparation, with the result that isolation can increase strains in their own personalities or in their family life.

What of the Future?

At first sight several factors point to decline. The population is small. It is unlikely to become any smaller, but there is little hope for expansion, partly because of a shortage of housing, especially for young families. Former sites of activity are all but desolate: the former railway-line at Waskerley has been turned into a bridlepath for horses and pedestrians, while at Ramshaw there is little but the remains of old mine-shafts and walls along the banks of the stream. There are fewer people on the land, while farms have become larger, and few farmers employ regular labour but rely instead on contract workers during peak periods. Owing to the height above sea-level—about 900 feet—the ground is not suitable for grain, and farmers depend upon cattle and sheep. But farmers are a sturdy breed, for you have to be sturdy to live in a hill area at the northern edge of the Pennines. Sons still continue to take over from their fathers, and many cannot visualise any other way of life.

The Tourists Are Coming!

One of the challenges at Blanchland both to the village and the church is that of tourism. The Lord Crewe Arms is the largest employer in the village; also the post office, village shop, tea room and art gallery are all dependent on visitors. In a historic village like Blanchland it is not easy to keep the balance between making the area attractive to tourists, and not allowing them to spoil the peaceful atmosphere.

I was interested to discover that, with very little publicity, about 10,000 people a year walk through Blanchland Abbey. Like other country parishes which receive visitors, we need to discover how best we can serve them. Why do people visit country churches? For mixed reasons, I believe; some are interested in history, some are enjoying a family day-out, while many are still looking for God in this confused world, and expect a country church in an attractive situation to proclaim something of Him.

How are we trying to serve visitors? First, by keeping the church open in daylight hours and making the building as attractive and informative as possible. A modern pictorial guide has been published, and a photographic exhibition is shown each summer, thanks to a local Heritage Centre which receives large grants from Manpower Services. We hope to produce a simple prayer leaflet in 1987, both for use by visitors and for sale on the bookstall, which last year sold over £2,000 worth of goods. Secondly, we are trying to be a welcoming church, both to individual visitors and also those who come on organised tours. In peak periods I try and be available for part of the day in the Abbey, and I hope to train one or two others to do the same.

We also welcome visiting parties for special services and a tour of the Abbey, who can be entertained afterwards by the ladies of the parish for tea. The profit from these teas is a very useful addition to the restoration fund. Contacts have been made with an outdoor centre for schools, which sometimes brings children to Blanchland, and we hope this year to provide white monks' costumes for schoolchildren to make their visit more interesting.

Ministry

And what of the life of the Church in this area, both in the present and the future? I have been priest-in-charge for just over two years and am still very much an apprentice. The problems are certainly becoming more clearly defined, while we are still searching for the answers. Decisions about the future will have to be taken by the Bishops of Newcastle and Durham, in consultation with diocesan pastoral committees and the parishes concerned. Should we remain as a group or not? Is the present group the right size? If we remain as a group, should we belong to the diocese of Newcastle or Durham? Answers will have to be found, and decisions made about deanery as well as diocesan boundaries.

Yet these questions do not reach the heart of the matter. Re-organisation is vital, but only part of the main concern of the church—the care of souls in each particular area. Many country parishes are very small in numbers, but every person matters in the sight of God, and the Church of England has responsibilities in every corner of the country. Whether the parish is large or small, urban or rural, we need to discover the most suitable way to minister to the people of each area.

Mention the word 'minister' to those in our area, and most people will think of the professional clergy, in spite of teaching and conferences and books that have been written about shared ministry. John Poulton in his recent book *Fresh Air* states the position very clearly—'Today we have to speak of parson and people. The development of the last centuries, and in particular the development of theology in the last hundred years, has been towards an emphasis on the laos of God, ie, the people of God (which includes the ordained ministry).' Yet in many a country parish, this is far from the reality. Some clergy find it very difficult to share their ministry, and some lay people are unwilling to accept new challenges. Traditional ideas have to be altered and strained relationships healed, before a new start can be made.

For the foreseeable future, at least, I believe that some form of professional ministry will be needed in our four parishes. There is the care of four scattered communities, as well as the tourist needs of the 10,000 people a year who visit Blanchland Abbey. An alternative to a full-time minister in the area would be one or more non-stipendiary ministers or else locally ordained ministers. Whichever method is used, it is vital for these ministers to understand and love the countryside.

Just as vital as the right choice of professional ministers is the choice and training of men and women from the local community to take their share in the total ministry of the church. To some extent this is already happening, as clergy who are responsible for several parishes can only live in one place, however much they travel. Churchwardens and church councillors are becoming more and more responsible for administration and finance, but the partnership of ministry needs to include spiritual as well as practical affairs. I used to work in Zimbabwe, where, together with an African colleague, I tried to serve 16 congregations in an area the size of Northumberland. A great deal depended on the local leaders, especially in African areas. They led Sunday worship, visited the sick, buried the dead and undertook basic instruction, while their clergy visited as frequently as they were able, depending upon seasonal rains, the latest security situation, petrol rationing and other difficulties. Could such local leaders in England be the salvation of the country church?

Bridge Building

In his sermon on July 17th, 1984, the Bishop of Newcastle outlined the task of 'bridge building'; building bridges between parishes and dioceses, building bridges between different groups and political parties, and building bridges between the community and God.

How well are our bridges being built? Parishioners are beginning to cross parochial and diocesan boundaries both for worship and social occasions. Once a month no morning service is held in Blanchland, and the congregation is encouraged to worship at Hunstanworth. Once a quarter, each parish takes it in turn to act as host to the others in the group, and we try to arrange a visiting preacher. I meet regularly with the churchwardens of all four parishes to discuss our programme and share ideas.

Publicity is important in every parish. We publish every month a locally produced magazine called *Crossroads* (four little parishes at the foot of the Cross), which is sent to all the homes in the area, and is much appreciated by the majority of readers.

Ecumenical relationships have been good in our area. Close co-operation continues with local Methodists. At Harvest time Blanchland Abbey, St James Hunstanworth, and Baybridge Chapel take turn to act as hosts for a united service, and on Christmas Eve Blanchland Abbey is usually packed with people from all three congregations as well as visitors. At Muggleswick united services are held with the local Catholics, and one of them serves on our church council.

Town parishes usually have a programme of weekday activities, but there is less need for them in small country parishes. Members of the congregation are also closely involved in the local community, and most of the village organisations are represented by someone in the congregation. Country shows are an important part of the agricultural year, and attract large crowds from near and far. Both my wife and I are involved in the local show at Blanchland.

In this chapter we have looked closely at the background of our four parishes, we have seen something of their history and geography, and discovered some of our failures and successes. God can speak to us in every situation, failure as well as success. As we look to the future, we need to keep our faith in God and his purpose for us all, especially in times of difficulty or doubt; at the same time we need to be firmly rooted in the realities of the present, whether at Blanchland or Hunstanworth, Edmundbyers or Muggleswick, or elsewhere.

'Speak, Lord', we say, 'your servants are listening.'

Chapter 5

Hedingham Baptist Fellowship Sible Hedingham, Essex

George Balfour

'Nothing changes here?'

George Balfour pastored the Hedingham Baptist Fellowship for twelve years, the latter four with the assistance of Roy Joslin. When George first came to Sible Hedingham in the early 1970s, attendance had dropped to 20 or 30, and there was serious talk of closing the church altogether. Gradually, through gentle, persistent encouragement, the Lord 'rebuilt the house': the leadership stabilised; finances became more secure; non-essential commitments were trimmed away; worship became more flexible; and the teaching and preaching ministry expanded. In an environment where nothing is supposed to change, here is a community that has slowly and quietly broken the rule!

George Balfour attended an Assemblies of God Bible College and then ministered in churches of various denominations. He has recently been invited to join the Rosebank Union Church in Johannesburg to commence a teaching ministry among the black pastors in South Africa. Gill, his wife, is a midwife. With her husband she enjoys walking, gardening and playing Scrabble! His son Mark is a student at York University and his daughter Rebecca is a trainee nurse in Cambridge.

Where are we?

The north-east Essex village of Sible Hedingham lies on the
main A604 between Colchester and Cambridge. In character it plays second fiddle to its more sophisticated
neighbour Castle Hedingham, a village famous for its well
preserved Norman keep and timber-framed buildings giving it an air of gentle old-world charm. Situated in an area
of England known for agriculture, it nevertheless has its
own industry as the home of a large timber and joinery firm
which until a few years ago was a family concern. Many of
the older inhabitants of the village are ex-employees. The
current population is in excess of 6,000 and growing as
further housing is erected to accommodate a commuting
workforce (and no doubt a future labour force for nearby
Stansted Airport which is due to become the Heathrow of
Essex). The village has two churches, Anglican and Baptist, still referred to as the church and the chapel.

The origins of the Old Baptist Chapel, as it was known,
date back from 1805, and a booklet published by a former
minister in 1928 relates something of the chequered and
turbulent history of the dissenting Baptist community. The
early founders recorded that their 'beginnings were small,
being at first but three who by reading the Scriptures were
convinced of the duty of Believers' Baptism'. These three
were at the time worshipping at an Independent Church in
Castle Hedingham. The love and graciousness of that
church were shown as, in dismissing the three members, the
church prayed 'that the God of all grace would abundantly
bless them and that they may all experience a growing con-
formity to the Image of the Son and hereafter join us in
communion with the Church triumphant in glory'. Quite a
lesson for many of us when losing members today!

The building, which we still use, was built at a cost of
£465. 19. 8½d. and was opened in July 1807. Members were
drawn from a radius of twelve miles around and soon churches
were planted out in the Suffolk towns of Haverhill and Sud-
bury. In the light of the present situation it seems that the Lord

built a firm foundation from which the future Fellowship
would develop.

The present chapter merely follows on and records God's
blessing and guiding through the last decade. At the time of
my arrival with my family in 1974, the church was in a state of
decline. Attendances had dropped to the extent that serious
consideration was being given to closing the church except
for a Sunday morning service. There appeared to be no clear
purpose ahead and no vision. The decline was not the fault
of the faithful few who prayed together and sought to keep
the doors open. Much heart-searching had been entered
into and a group of younger men held the diaconate together. It is not easy to pinpoint the reasons for the state of
the church at that time. Ministry had been supplied by faithful laymen who, despite their willingness to lead worship
and preach the Word, could not, by virtue of their itinerant
nature, bring direction and vision to what seemingly was a
lost cause. The membership at this time was 36, though for
practical purposes, because of old age or other good reason,
it was nearer 20. There was a small Boys' Brigade group, a
Sunday school serving a handful of children, and a Ladies'
meeting once a week on a Tuesday afternoon. Finances
were low and attendance on Sundays ranged from 20 to 30 in
a morning (including children) to 8 to 10 in the evening. All
in all a daunting prospect, particularly as it was following the
general trend in the area with chapels fighting against apathy
and decaying buildings. The enthusiasm and zeal which had
planted the village churches had somehow died with the
pioneers, and the torch had not been handed on.

This was not my first attempt at village work. The previous five years had been spent as a lay pastor to a small village church in Black Notley, about 12 miles away to the east
of Braintree. This church figures later in the present record.

What Gives?

January 1974 saw a rather reluctant pastor begin what was to
prove to be the most joyful and rewarding years of ministry

that I had ever experienced. The first seven years were to be spent in a lay capacity while I pursued a career in planning administration in Chelmsford, and the latter five as the full-time pastor as the church grew numerically, spiritually and financially. Around me initially was a tiny band of people of all ages who had placed their faith in God and their hope in me, believing that there was a future together. It was hard to see clearly what should be the starting point.

The meetings for worship were sparsely attended; strangers coming in would quickly assess the situation and move on again. It was not that we were not worshipping the Lord, nor that our hearts were not open to His Spirit, but there was a lack of vitality. 'Nothing changes here' were not only words of a beautiful hymn, but prophetically true of our coming together, each meeting being a replica of the last, hopefully with the exception of the sermon! The building did not help—rotting floorboards, noisy gas heaters, peeling paintwork—it gave shelter and comfort to spiders and the like but not to aspiring children of the Lord. The pulpit bathed in former glory; Charles Spurgeon had once preached from it and seemingly was put off from ever coming again!

It all sounds so dull and depressing, and in human terms it was. There was, however, a spark of life and expectancy in the heart of the people. I recognised that each one was precious in the sight of the Lord and had no desire to take the church by storm and leave casualties strewn along the wayside on the pretext that they 'did not want to go on with God'. I did not subscribe to the view, nor do I now, that in the cause of renewal we may lose people. It is sometimes suggested that it is the inevitable price to be paid and has a particular reference in some minds to the elderly. But I valued highly the steadfast doggedness of some of the senior members who though they were not in fact resistant to change were anxious to know that the Lord was being honoured. I respected their wisdom, and I believe much potential has been lost by adopting a cavalier attitude to the senior citizens of the Kingdom.

In fact I had cherished a dream that had at that time not

been realised: that one day I would pastor a church contain-
ing three generations of families committed to the Lord. It
was a target worth aiming for. Two further emphases were
in my heart which found acceptance with the deacons and
the people. One was in the planting of churches where
there was no witness, and the other the fostering of a meaningful missionary focus. These then were the early struggles
and the subject of much sharing and praying with those who
were at first reluctant co-leaders. However, they quickly
stood in their place as they began to be encouraged in God.

Unless the Lord Build the House ...

So began the building process of this church in rural Essex.
I asked for the men who were deacons on my arrival to be
allowed to stay in office for a three-year period. At that
time deacons were voted in on a rota basis for three years,
and this could have meant a total change of leadership before we had consolidated. Thankfully, all were in agreement and I believe this move put in a firm foundation for
progress. Prayer and openness of thought became the
keynote of those early leaders' meetings. We were all learning together, and I look back with deep affection on those
days. Often our meetings would begin with solemn inter-
cession, continue with necessary business and end in much
laughter and warmth. God was indeed among us!

One of the first decisions we made was with reference to
finance. The annual budget was around £700, a small
amount, but the Lord's to direct where it should go. Good
stewardship was essential, and we wanted to give as well as
receive. It was decided therefore to recommend that a tithe
of all our monies should be earmarked for overseas work.
We also agreed that finance would never become a priority
in either our leaders' meetings or members' meetings. God
would supply what he could trust us with, and we believed
that we would never be bound in our outreach and work by
lack of funds. Declare the vision as the Lord gives it and the
wherewithal would be added. It worked then and it still

works. To this day not a penny is raised through special efforts, and money remains a low priority in our meetings together. Yet we have never lacked for anything.

What's Essential?

We also began to consider which aspects of the work we had inherited were actually essential. It could be argued that all were, but we were sure that there was a case for review and pruning. As churches grow, meetings proliferate; workers become tired and dispirited especially if their own area of work is not 'successful' and an administrative but ineffective monster is birthed. When we forget why something has commenced it is time to consider whether it should continue. Not that we had a massive commitment. Apart from Sundays there was the tiny Sunday school, a midweek Bible study/prayer meeting, a Ladies' afternoon meeting (at which the gospel was and still is faithfully preached to those who would not otherwise hear it) and a spluttering attempt to keep a children's meeting alive. The children actually *were*—alive—it was the workers who were the cause for concern! It was largely an exercise to keep the evangelical flame burning, but the ashes were growing cold. Attendance was on an 'if I feel like it' level and there was little purpose apart from keeping it all going, and little sense of expectation. In such circumstances those leading such groups become jaded and dispirited. They also often feel guilty because if they were truthful they would resign from their position but dare not because no one would take their place.

We asked the Lord about this, especially about the children's work. Another conviction of mine then, one which still remains, is that a church does not grow on the strength of a children's work, however commendable it might seem. I had often observed that in the frantic attempts to evangelise the children, not only had money and man hours become disproportionate to the rest of the needs but also the actual remaining fruit over the years was negligible. In our case we felt it right to close down all the children's work as it then was and to recommence a ministry to our own members' children. It was a 'beginning at Jerusalem' principle. This move was, of course, controversial, and not without some heartache. Surely our primary call was to spread the Word among the village children? Nevertheless we took our stand and began to care for the six children who at that time were the sum total of our church offspring. The result has been that over the years we have seen young children who gave their hearts to the Lord still remaining in the church, though now at universities and work.

We also gently but firmly dismantled the Boys' Brigade, also the mid-week meeting for prayer and Bible study, re-designating it as a prayer meeting only. Teaching of the World was reserved for Sundays. We determined that any future meetings would only be commenced if a need was felt, and if that need was matched by those who had an inescapable call from God to lead. The old theory that one recruits workers (evidence of breathing will do) to a static and often stagnant church programme—only to release them in death or the Rapture—was abandoned!

Future workers would also be given an escape route from the treadmill of service. As needs changed and as their own emphasis or responsibilities evolved, it was necessary to give them a hope for honourable withdrawal, without attendant guilt. Hence we built in an understanding that they would serve for a period of two years, at the end of which they and we could review the situation. This has prevented monopolies and bottlenecks over the years and has allowed for flexibility and freshness.

Patterns of Worship

My own attention was engaged in bringing the change into ministry and worship. I had always considered those as my responsibility and had conducted both almost exclusively. From time to time others would preach, but it was mainly my prerogative. Now I began to see that things would have to change and that I would have to be flexible. Questions came to my mind, and I struggled with them. How could I entrust these roles to others? What if things went wrong, where would the responsibility lie? I had been asked to take the role of the overseer; should I not therefore be seen to be 'over'?

The transition was not easy for me, but gradually I began to see that while the burden of the teaching ministry would have to be mine for the time being, at least until others emerged, it was not so with worship. Here was a 'specialist' area. It was not a matter of compiling the menu of the day to contain my favourite hymns, or even choruses. Here was a ministry which required a great measure of dedication and sensitivity as well as musical skills and understanding. There was a man gifted in this way in the church. The fact that Fred Daborn was also a deacon made it easier for me to thrust him into the forefront. Fred began gently and with much dedication to lead us into new avenues of expression. He is still doing so.

New patterns evolved rather than radically arriving overnight. People began to respond to the confidence they found in Fred by a new-found assurance and confidence in themselves. Many of the renewal songs helped but so also did the grand old hymns that confirm so well the ground of truth in which every Christian must ultimately stand secure. The burden was to make the worship not only lively but relevant. 'Lively' was not necessarily interpreted by arm signals or the latest soft shoe shuffle, though I hasten to add these were not frowned upon. The whole aim was to allow individuals to be themselves. We remembered the teaching of the Apostle Paul that just one member could make the rest suffer, and Christian courtesy was the order of the day. I believe that by proceeding that way we avoid inflicting too many wounds though I am sure we were not without some offence. Some were threatened by the new-found liberty which to them meant not having a hymn board and sometimes singing a chorus three times instead of the statutory twice.

We were swiftly labelled 'charismatic' presumably because we did not follow the usual format, which incidentally we never condemned but simply discarded as not the way for us. Certainly the label could not stick because of any emphasis on spiritual gifts. While teaching on gifts was part of the curriculum and some of us did speak in tongues in the privacy of our own prayer life—or sometimes in the fervency of the mid-week meeting—Sundays for the time being seemed to be out of bounds for the Holy Spirit in this way. Why this was I am not sure, except that we were not out to rock the secure boats of some, nor gain a reputation from others.

Things have now changed somewhat, and Sunday gatherings nowadays would include the prophetic word (duly weighed), singing in the Spirit, an occasional tongue with interpretation, and a suitable balance of the operation of the Word of Wisdom and the Word of Knowledge. The sick and the sad are also prayed for regularly, and while we could not make any great claim to constant miracles, we have seen God at work in people's lives, for which we give thanks. These miracles were gentle and lovely beginnings when the love of Christ was evident among us in binding us together. A trickle and then a small stream of people began to join us.

Teaching

The other ministry area, that of teaching, became my own focal point. Happy to leave the worship leading to others more capable and gifted than I, I began to bring consecutive teaching into the fellowship. Mornings became family teaching times as I tackled practical issues of everyday Christian living. The evenings, however, continued to be a problem both in attendance and aim. Whatever persuasion we used, it seemed unreal to expect people to turn out to what was more or less a repeat performance of the morning minus the children, albeit with a different Word. Tradition said that the evening was a 'gospel meeting'. I have never been sure why we expect unbelievers to turn out on a Sunday night; the truth in my experience is that they do not. A diet of John 3:16 in varied guises is no formula for growth for a church, and I began to address myself to the problem.

It was a few years before we eventually took the radical step of changing the timing of the evening meeting from 6.30 pm to 7.00 pm and at the same time declared it to be open-ended. In fact we aimed for 9.00 pm as a limit, though did not make that time sacrosanct in our minds. We had stumbled along the pathway of 7.30 pm finish and then the so-called 'after-church meetings'. They were neither one thing nor the other and seemed to cater only for a few young people who were bent on drinking coffee and eating the remains of the cakes baked for Sunday tea. Pleasant but hardly progressive. If there was a need for an 'after church' then why should it not be 'in church'? The change was made, and a determined pathway of directional teaching was opened up. Sunday evening rapidly became the more eagerly attended and has continued to be so. Much of the progress that has been made can be attributed to that particular move with people coming together, committed to worshipping, praying and listening as one.

The Communion Table

Coinciding with those changes came a very clear conviction that the meaning of the Communion table should become more central. The practice, as in many Baptist churches, was to take Communion twice a month, once in an evening and once in a morning. It was also customary for opportunity to be given for people to leave the service after the benediction and then for those remaining to celebrate the act of Remembrance. I think we are guilty of underestimating the powerful influence and witness of the Communion Service. In the book of Acts and in the history of the Early Church there seemed to be a greater emphasis and regard for the Communion table than certainly we were giving it by relegating it to a bi-monthly 'participate-if-you-like' invitation. At its inception in the Feast of the Passover, it was enacted by Israel and observed by the Egyptians and was no doubt a profound and powerful witness to the presence and redemptive purposes of God. So it appeared to us that we ought to consider gathering in this way more often. The intention would not be to make it an everyday occurrence, thereby robbing it of any significance, but to use the act both as a central point of worship and also as an evangelical witness. We therefore decided to prepare the table for every Sunday gathering. This practice has now continued for the best part of five years and we see no reason to change. It has been a place of healing both physical and relational. A number have found the challenge of participating unbearable because of their unbelief. Through it they have come to know Christ as Saviour and Lord, often making their commitment during the eating of the bread and the drinking of the wine. This has been remarkably the case among teenagers. Far from becoming ordinary, the Communion has become extraordinary in its effect upon us all.

Growth and Change

The growth in the fellowship, slow at first, has rapidly increased particularly during the past three years when membership has risen from about 60 to over 150 today. In addition we minister to a further 100 adults in the meetings and have over 100 children in the Junior Church. These figures are realistic, because we have an annual renewal of membership which has been done for the past three years. True membership was always a difficult thing to estimate. The church roll often needs saving from the sin of exaggeration and even untruth. Often members are still listed who have long ago been promoted, as they say, to glory! While such a cloud of witnesses is still valid according to Scripture, there is a remarkable lack of enthusiasm from such when it comes to earthly toil and care! So we set about putting it to rights and on a day in 1982 declared permanent membership a thing of the past. All existing members were dismissed with the opportunity of signing on again for a year with the definite objective of supporting the work and the leaders. Most came back and willingly signed on. One or two objected at the time but thankfully have now accepted the principle. The result has been that the Annual General Meeting each year is a meaningful one with an act of love and fellowship as we join hands and hearts for another year in the cause of the gospel. This has had a twofold effect. The first is that it means that the leadership is assured of continued support to carry out the programme of work. The second is that it gives all members an opportunity to lapse without confrontation leading to leaving the church altogether. Someone may have a very good reason for not being entirely sure of the way a church is going but still want to maintain friendships and fellowship. That can now be done by the simple process of standing down from membership for a time. We then visit the person to seek to understand the reason why and if possible to learn something new. This has proved to be healthy and workable.

Growth patterns are always interesting for analysis and comment. Any responsible leadership will be aware of these and will surely lament if the major growth does not eventually come from new converts. In the beginning it has to be confessed that we saw many people coming in from other churches. There is not, of course, quite the choice in a rural situation that there is in a city, but it was never our intention to promote growth in this way. We tried to build safeguards and sought to act with other churches in the area to prevent loss and gain on minor pretexts. History shows that we often failed badly. Our intentions were good, but the carrying out of them was not always effective and we sometimes hurt other congregations. This we regret and ask forgiveness where we have been less than perfect. Some people were drawn in for their own personal reasons—some valid and some selfish. If they came because they felt we were more 'lively', then they soon found out that there is more to belonging than joining in the Sunday celebration. There are six other days of the week to live. Some perhaps thought we were able to care better. God will be the final judge of these and all other motives and will be the One to forgive where we have failed to live up to the reputation others would give to us but which we have often been unable to attain.

In any event, we are now seeing a much larger proportion of new converts, which must surely please the Lord. It certainly pleases us. Discipleship is a high priority, and we constantly seek to bring these new 'babes' from the 'milk' stage to 'meat'. All who signify their desire to be part of the fellowship, whether converts or not, are required to attend an induction course for a period of ten weeks. No one can be brought into membership without attending. In it we ensure that the way of salvation is shown, some basic teaching on prayer and Bible reading is given, and then a clear declaration of the intent of the fellowship together with its stand on baptism, spiritual gifts, finance and outreach is given. Finally, the meaning of membership is explained, and at the end of that course an invitation to join is given. I know this is not unique, and many other churches have a similar programme. Where such an induction course is offered, invariably a more meaningful membership is produced. It ensures, if nothing else, that no one just slips in without knowing fully the implications.

Finances have also increased with the passage of time and we still maintain a low profile in this area. We record with deep gratitude the faithfulness of God and the expression of his faithfulness through the generosity of the people. Our annual budget which for the current year (1986) will be in the region of £40,000, has enabled us to reach out in many ways. Missionary giving has increased from 10% to 15% and will rise to 20% during 1987. We have also been able to allocate considerable sums for church planting, evangelism and the release of men into ministry.

This year, after twelve years of service to the fellowship, the Lord has given me a clear call to work in South Africa. Much of the detail is yet to be worked out, but the church has blessed us as a family by committing themselves to adequate financial support to enable me to pursue a ministry without concern in that respect. They see me as their first missionary. It is also a novel way of getting rid of the pastor! In my place they have accepted Roy Joslin, a young man who has served faithfully alongside me for a number of years. He is one of the congregation, and God has clearly laid it on his heart to shepherd his people. It has been a joy to see him progress and now take the pastoral role. He will be supported full-time.

Increased finance has also meant we have been able to clear the church building of its rotting wood and famous pulpit to make it a more useful building suited to the updated purposes of God for us. Additionally we have also replaced a decrepit schoolroom by a new extension, and all debts are paid in full.

Inevitably with the years the patterns of leadership have changed because pressure and responsibility demanded it. Deacons became Elders, approved by the membership on the recommendations of the pastor. Deacons as such disappeared. By that I mean the old system of voting for a man then finding a job for him. The trend today in our situation is to recognise certain tasks as diaconal roles and then to recognise that the person doing it is a deacon.

A further extension of shared leadership, probably unacceptable to some, is to recognise the wives as 'helpmeets'. Perhaps that sounds not too unscriptural after all. Generally we have found this to be a strength and to be commended, and for our wives to meet and pray over our agendas before the men meet is an encouraging thing. I suspect too that at times such prayer meetings have changed our minds, although we would never want to confess that publicly, now would we?

Outreach

One criticism, valid in part, is that for a number of years we did not carry out any evangelism, nor did we touch the social needs of the area. There were several reasons. One was the feeling that we needed to consolidate for a time before we stretched out in other areas. Then there was the fact that

our catchment area had spread beyond the local village to a
twenty-mile radius incorporating at least a dozen other villages and this meant thinking through our policy carefully.
Obviously someone travelling in for twenty miles could not
be expected to have the same concern for Sible Hedingham
as those who actually lived there. The steady growth also
meant that evangelism in any aggressive form might mean
that our already overcrowded premises would not be able
to cope. Out of this happy predicament house groups were
born. The intention was for them to be caring groups in
each area under dedicated leadership, linking in to the
centre but having a large measure of autonomy. Our prayer
was that out of that strategy the Lord would show us when
and where to plant churches, which was my desire from the
very beginning. The Lord has been gracious to us in this
way, and our first church planting was back into the village
of Black Notley. This was particularly exciting for me as it
was the place in which I had laboured prior to my call to
Sible Hedingham. The congregation there had dwindled to
just four people. Today, three years later, it has a membership of 25 and a congregation of 60–70 with a small but
thriving Sunday school; it will not be long before it becomes
an independent fellowship. We have also hired village halls
and at least four other areas are showing clear potential for
further church planting. Evangelism, in the accepted sense
of that word, has not been carried out; nevertheless, the
Lord has added and we are open to his leading us in this
way.

The social impact is also beginning, especially in Sible
Hedingham. A telephone 'Helpline' set up to assist any in
distress is proving a most fruitful way of showing our care in
practical ways. Other projects to help the aged and the
handicapped are also being carefully monitored, and one of
the elders makes this his full-time concern. We believe that
a church must not only preach the gospel but live it, too.
Our efforts are sometimes feeble, but at least we are having
a go and believe that the Lord will honour our efforts. What
we do in Sible Hedingham will we pray be done in the
church-planting areas. We pray too that what the Lord has

done among us by his grace will be a provocative challenge to others who at this time are faithfully keeping the doors open and sometimes feel like giving up.

What does the future hold for our church? Leaving it has been a painful process for me in some ways. It has been the central point of my life for so long as together with my wife, Gill, we have endeavoured to serve the Lord. One of the saddest sights in all the earth is to see places that once were alive and thriving become sepulchres, and I pray that this will never be the case here. I firmly believe that the Holy Spirit multiplies, but it is the Devil who divides. As long as this, or any church, will give out as they receive, willing to submit their programmes and their progress to the Lord, then God will honour faithfulness. The opportunities in the rural areas are enormous.

May Sible Hedingham, and those like it, be a part of a mighty move of God among the forgotten villages of this beloved country.

Chapter 6

Bellingham Methodist United Reformed Church, Northumberland

Peter Wright

'We shall try to love them better'

Rural depopulation is something Peter Wright is constantly battling against in his area. He is a Free Church minister with pastoral charge of nine Methodist and four United Reformed churches—a task which no one would undertake lightly! Yet the joy and hope that shine through this chapter are encouragements to rural and city church-goers alike. Any differences between Methodist and United Reformed thinking have been thrown to the wind, as a spirit of unity determines to make its mark on village life in the North Tyne valley. The church continues to be a focal point for the local people—as in most rural areas—in a way that has long been forgotten in towns and cities. Religious feeling runs deep in rural communities, and Peter Wright has undertaken, with the aid of his congregations, to reach out with love to those who apparently shun the faith.

Peter went to Wesley Theological College as a mature student. He has a wife—Jaqueline—and two adult children. His hobbies include computers, snooker, cooking and walking —but most of all he enjoys being happy!

Setting and History

Imagine 800 square miles of rolling upland moorland, slashed down the middle by a clean, salmon-filled river, dotted with some 20 small communities of fewer than 900 souls (and in most cases fewer than 200), all of whom are warm-hearted, generous and violently independent, and you have a fair picture of the North Tyne valley in Northumberland.

As the Free Church minister with pastoral charge of the nine Methodist and four United Reformed churches that serve the area, I find some difficulty in selecting just one on which to focus attention for the purpose of talking about rural church life. In order to be fair to the situation, I feel obliged to begin by giving a résumé of the total church situation as I found it upon my arrival in the early autumn of 1980.

Within the area, there were two Roman Catholic churches (at Bellingham and Otterburn) both being served by the priest resident in Bellingham, who also held services in the local community centre in the remote village of Kielder. The Roman Catholic folk of the lower reaches of the valley tended to gravitate to the large church at Hexham which is outside the area under consideration.

The Church of England was served by 8 clergy who between them had pastoral responsibility for 18 churches. The area was administered in two parts; the BOG (the Bellingham-Otterburn Group), a pseudo-team ministry; and the other part being the remaining lower North Tyne churches.

The United Reformed Church was in the pastoral care of two clergy, one of whom lived at Birdhopecraig and had charge of the churches at Birdhopecraig/Otterburn/West Woodburn. The other lived in Bellingham and had charge of the North Tyne Group whch comprised Bellingham/Wark/Falstone/Kielder.

My own Methodist appointment was to serve the nine churches scattered along the North Tyne and Rede valley, two of them situated down on the South Tyne ... (not a lot if you say it quickly!).

As I write, the situation has changed greatly since 1980. One of the greatest agents for change has been financial pressure, with the problem of clergy shortage following a close second.

The Roman Catholic church has not seen any changes in its pattern of services or serving clergy, and as the members are not particularly poor it is unlikely that any real change will occur in the foreseeable future.

The Church of England has had to make some sacrifices in the manning levels it has previously enjoyed. The area now only has six clergy, and is even at this moment considering reducing still further to five or even four!

The United Reformed Church (which here in the 'Not-England-Not-Scotland-area' between the Scottish border and Hadrian's Wall still thinks of itself as being the Presbyterian Church) maintains its minister at Otterburn, but since 1982 has had a joint work, in the upper reaches of the North Tyne, with the Methodist Church.

What happened was that when the URC man in Bellingham came to retirement age, the churches and the district council had to examine seriously the financial considerations in inviting a man to serve four churches in a remote area with a combined membership of less than eighty! At an early stage in the discussion, it was noted that the Methodist Church already covered the area pastorally and that they too were very concerned about the problems of serving very scattered small communities. The outcome was that they approached me as the minister at that time, to consider the possibility of taking on the pastoral oversight of the North Tyne Group of the URC.

After very thoughtful and prayerful consultation with the Circuit staff and the Chairman of the District, it was agreed that such a scheme might be of benefit to both churches, and so in May of 1982, I was inducted and became 'recognised and regarded' as a United Reformed Church minister with pastoral charge of the North Tyne Group.

Bellingham

Of all the churches in the Methodist and URC groupings,

the strongest in both cases were located in the central village of Bellingham. It is upon the church in Bellingham that we shall concentrate. But first let me sketch in some background information about the North Tyne and the area that centres upon Bellingham.

Since the last war (and I suspect that to a lesser extent, even before then), rural depopulation has been occurring at the rate of 40% per decade! The causes are not difficult to dig out.

Farm mechanisation

At the turn of the century, every farm would have been almost a hamlet in itself. Apart from the farmer and his immediate family (and families then were much larger than today) there would have been three or four farm labourers, each with a wife and several children, a community of maybe thirty souls or more. Of course, there were horses to be handled and hay, cereals, straw and root crops which would require the services of even more labour employed on a casual basis. Today, this and more is done by the farmer, with perhaps a son and one general farm worker who is usually a 'tractorman' or 'shepherd' or 'cowman' or some other 'specialist' who has a whole range of machines to hand, all of which are able to do the work of many people.

The net result is that whereas the 'farm' used to be a small thriving community in its own right, it is now more often than not a single house, too large for the farmer's needs. And to cap it all, the farm hands probably live miles away and come in each morning by car!

The Forestry Commission

Since the 1930s, the North Tyne has been developed as the largest man-made forest in Europe (centred upon Kielder) through the efforts of the Forestry Commission. This made the Commission one of the largest employers in the area.

The Forestry Commission developed several small villages, as it could not envisage that there would ever be a day when they would not need armies of men to cut and haul trees ... and then came that incredible invention, the portable one-man chainsaw. Almost overnight, the Commission found itself having to reduce the workforce. Nowadays, the villages are half empty, and some of the houses (all owned by the Commission) are even being used to store fir cones!

Add to farm mechanisation and the cut-back in forestry work the fact that we 'train' our children to leave the rural areas for schooling, entertainment, social contacts and job prospects—and you will see how in many ways the countryside is becoming a sparsely populated geriatric community without benefit of necessary services such as buses and shops.

All of this militates against church life.

A Solution for the Churches

From the moment that it was agreed that the URC North Tyne Group should 'merge' with the North Tyne Section of the Hexham Circuit of the Methodist Church, it became obvious that the two separate churches in Bellingham could and should work towards becoming one congregation.

The URC building was on the edge of the village, and although of a similar size and usefulness to the Methodist property, it was in need of some fairly extensive renovation, not to mention a radical review of its heating system.

A further problem was that the church was approached by a hill which proved a real trouble to some of the older folk.

The Methodist property was however situated in the centre of the village on comparatively flat ground, and was agreed to be the most convenient and suitable.

At a meeting within the first month of the 'shared pastorate' the URC folk graciously agreed to unite in worship and service in the Methodist premises for a trial period of a year, with the express intention of seeking ways of bringing the two congregations into a harmonious union which did not deny either tradition. At this time, on paper, the URC membership was 38 and the Methodist membership 33, but the actual attendances were more often than not less than a dozen in either church.

Theologically, there is very little difference between the URC and the Methodist Church and almost all the 'differences' were centred in administration. There was no fundamental disagreement on matters of faith, or even on interpretation of Scripture.

The group that worked together to seek the way forward soon agreed that if some way of ensuring that the 'spirit' of the 'Basis of Union and the Structure of the United Reformed Church' and 'The Constitutional Practice and Discipline of the Methodist Church' could in some way be enshrined in one agreed method of working, then a large step would have been taken towards genuine unity.

The outcome of the meetings of this group and some extensive study of the detailed requirements of each of these documents was an agreed agenda for two meetings per year. This agreement sought to fulfil all that the 'law' required in both denominations.

The two agendas proved to the leaders of both churches that with just a little give and take, it was possible to deal with all the 'business' of the church on a joint basis, and that where matters legally demanded that they be dealt with in a denominational manner, this could easily be done in the same meeting with the 'others' not taking part in any voting. Even so, it was agreed that *all* matters should be discussed in the open meeting, regardless of the subject or content.

It might be worthwhile at ths point to reproduce the text of the preamble to the printed and agreed 'Agendas':

> The 'Joint Church Meeting' shall comprise, for
> all the ordinary workings of the Church and its
> general management, all duly elected members
> of the (Methodist) Church Council and the

appointed members of the (URC) Management Committee.

The 'ordinary workings' of the Church shall be deemed to be those printed in the 'Agendas' on the pages which follow for the 'Autumn' and 'Spring' Meetings each year.

Matters relating to the week by week running and concerns of the Church may be brought up at these meetings either under the appropriate captions or under 'Any Other Business', but matters which affect the fundamental nature of the Bellingham Methodist United Reformed Church (eg: the 'Call' to a Minister; basic policy of the Church—local or national; proposals of a radical nature etc) shall be proper cause for a Joint Members' Meeting to be called.

The Annual Meeting of Members shall in any case be held concurrent with the Autumn Joint Church Meeting.

The 'Agendas' have been prepared in order that the constitutional requirements of both the United Reformed Church and the Methodist Church shall be met. The references against each item refer to the Constitutional Practice and Discipline of the Methodist Church (CPD), and the Basis of Union and the Structure of the United Reformed Church (BU).

As the whole of our being together is a 'growing and developing' relationship, it is to be noted that the 'Agendas' following are not intended as exhaustive or exclusive, but are there as a guide in our search for an effective and amicable life together.

As we discover the need for change in our patterns of administration and behaviour, so we hope by discussion and prayer to find the right way through for this community of God's people.

It was in this mood of openness and faith that the joint venture began in May 1982.

A year later, resulting from a motion that came spontaneously from the floor at the spring 1983 meeting, the church made formal and legal application to become a joint Methodist United Reformed Church (MURC), under the 1969 Act.

Before application was made, every member/adherent/friend of the two churches was asked to vote on a ballot paper as to whether or not they favoured this 'marriage'. There was a 95% response, and not one single negative or neutral vote among them. Those who did not respond were then seen personally and asked if they objected. No one did! In fact the opposite was the case, with great encouragement voiced by everyone.

From that point, it took a further two years to go through all the legal channels and various courts of the two churches but, on 16th June 1985, at a celebratory service, the final documents were signed in the church.

Can These Dry Bones Live?

Of course, during the time between the URC folk first entering the building and that moment of final signing, there had been a tremendous growth of fellowship and sharing and week by week worship and learning together.

The meetings of the Joint Council were exceedingly friendly and although at first there was a natural caution about the way each other did various things, nonetheless, with great sensitivity to each other's traditions and practices, the two groups of leaders gradually came to trust each other and accept each others' points of view.

One of the early discussions revolved around the introduction of Beetle Drives, which the URC folk had always enjoyed as a social event. The Methodist folk were very much aware of Methodism's staunch stand against gambling. In the end, it was agreed that an experimental Drive would be held but that only small token prizes would be given. (Under the terms of the Sharing of Church Buildings Act, 1969, whenever an event of URC origin or organisation takes place, the building is deemed for the duration of that event to be completely URC property and therefore able to be used for whatever practices are acceptable on URC premises.) The 'tail-piece' to all this is that most of the prizes were won by Methodists!

The Beginnings of Life

One of the most effective efforts to bring the local folk into the church has been the introduction of family worship which is held on the first Sunday in every month.

Prior to the joining, neither church had a viable ministry to children. With the introduction of the family service, attendance on the first Sunday increased to around 90! This has now—some four years later—levelled off at around 65/70 each month. The split is about 50/50 children/adults.

The service is geared entirely to the needs of the children, who range in age between 4 and 14, and the rest of the congregation has been made aware that they are there to 'ride on the coat-tails of the children' (the reverse being the case at services designed to cater for adults). I'm not sure whether it's a compliment or not, but the comment that comes quite often from some of the elderly members who attend family service is, 'Well I got more from that than I do from most sermons, Peter!'

It's interesting to note that we are unable to keep our children after 14, when they start attending the high school some 15 miles away from the village. We hope of course that by then we have done most of our work and that what has been shared with them will provide a good foundation.

Attendance on 'normal' Sundays is between 18 and 24, which is still an increase on the previous sum of the two separate congregations, and of course we are deeply aware that many of our folk are involved in agriculture, which is not only very demanding but recognises no day of rest. We are also very conscious that many of our members are getting frail with the passing years and are unable to face the rigours of the journey to their beloved 'chapel'. Even so, the leadership of the church is concerned that folk turn out for specials such as Harvest and family service, but find it impossible to attend regularly otherwise.

That there is potential for growth within Bellingham cannot be denied, even though the village population is only around 850. After counting those who are definitely connected to either the Roman Catholic Church, the Anglican Church or our own MURC, there is still about a third of the village on whom we have very little effect. I am careful not to say that we have 'no effect', for that would not be true. Village life is such that when the majority of people are inter-related in some way or other, whatever one does is bound to have repercussions in the wider community. Perhaps this is an indication of one of the great strengths of rural life and an advantage it has over suburbia ... it has a real understanding of what it means to *live in community*.

Having written earlier on in this chapter about some of the factors that militate *against* the life of the Church in the North Tyne, let me now, based on my Bellingham experience, regale you with some of the factors that I see working *in favour* of the life of the church.

Tradition

In my experience tradition goes deeper and holds longer in the countryside than it does in the town. Within the life of the rural community, church life is still, if not *the* focus, one of the foci (along with the National Farmers' Union, Young Farmers' Club and the Pony Club, which always seem to meet on a Sunday!). The church may find strength in this fact, especially if it can shape itself to the needs of the people—for example, it needs to be prepared to lovingly excuse farmers from all church affairs at lambing time. It needs to realise that deep down in the rural psyche is a very resilient thread of joyful paganism which rises up in the guise of Christianity at harvest, Christmas, baptisms and funerals.

One of the most popular of all the services we hold each year is the Celebration of Nine Lessons and Carols, when we are able to fill the church *and* crush the hall to capacity, due in no small measure to the atmosphere created by the judicious use of candlelight and mince pies.

We delight in all this because it gives us an opportunity to share the essential matters of faith, and the carrot—even in the shape of mince pie!—is of very secondary importance.

The Reality of Community

Within the churches, there is an interlinked community of care that spreads out into the entire community and in so doing creates an environment in which there are no anonymous people. This is seen in the fact that every committee in the village that has even the slightest hint of a task that could be described as 'good' has at least one or more of our people serving on it. In a small community, the impact of a slight but significant percentage of the people (ie the church) is far greater than in the city where the church may become a 'holy huddle', overwhelmed by the hordes of anonymous people around it.

Creation and the Church

There is also what I can only call a sense of the givenness of creation. It's no old wives' tale that those who live close to the earth have a more immediate sense of God in the teeming life of nature. The real benefit of such a simple and close relationship is that the potential for a 'God-centred community' is so much greater. I find all this to be true, not only in Bellingham but in all the churches and communities that I serve within the North Tyne valley in general, and that fact gives me great hope.

What of the Future?

I feel it would be foolish to examine such a question with the prior intention of trying to assess possible 'successes' or 'failures', because that's not the name of the game.

All our paths into the future are at this moment only lines of possibilities. So many factors (of which we are unaware or which do not even yet exist) may influence the way we go, that to talk of success or failure is nonsense.

I believe though that we *can* talk about 'viable intentions' which are based on a combination of our present knowledge, the way we instinctively apply our faith and our corporate relationship with God.

In the case of Bellingham, our present knowledge includes the following facts: we are a numerically shrinking community; we are an ageing community; we are being progressively deprived of services such as shops, buses and community aid. All of this suggests that the small rural communities will be more and more thrown back on their own resources with the minority of able-bodied people caring for the majority old and infirm. This pattern has already emerged in Bellingham and continues to develop.

Faith But Not Faith

There is also a very real implicit faith among the people and I do include those formally outside the church. That faith is not one that the people find it easy to put into words, and it has strands of emotionalism tied up with childhood memories of family church involvement. But beneath all those things, I believe there is a sense of identity with those who do take themselves along to their church on a Sunday.

Perhaps that is why those who shout loudest when a chapel has to close are those who are least likely to attend! Closing a chapel implies that 'God has abandoned us'.

This 'implicit faith' probably forms the basis for what I see as the corporate relationship with God. It is true that there are those for whom the idea of 'God' has no basis in reality, but they are very few and far between in the country areas. During six years of browsing through the admissions register at the General Hospital which serves the North Tyne valley, I have only *once* come across an entry where the patient has declared himself to be 'atheist', and not one entry for an agnostic. I don't believe that it stretches the point too far to say that there is a communal faith that has very little to do with denominations, doctrine or dogma, but that might gently fumble its way through the Apostles Creed with a little scratching of the head in parts, and say 'amen' at the end.

The Ground of Hope

All of this gives me hope! Not of massive evangelical revivals—not of vastly increased congregations—but of the Kingdom of God quietly growing in the hearts of ordinary people, living out a simple, loving faith in what is one of the finest examples of community that I have ever experienced in this or any of the other countries in which I have been.

There will always be those who want to exclude them-selves from the Kingdom, through ignorance or fear, but here in Bellingham and the North Tyne, we shall try (as we used to say to the child who had fallen down) to 'love them better'.

Chapter 7

The Swanborough Team, Wiltshire

Richard Askew

'Most miracles come quietly'

The Reverend John Whettem is head of the Swanborough Team, a group of nine churches from eight villages in the Swanborough area. The team works together to establish a unity of vision as well as deeper pastoral care and mutual support. John Whettem's aim has been to offer a range of worship styles for different tastes, bringing together the more traditional and the more progressive in the process. Starting from an emphasis on 'neighbourliness', these villages in the Wiltshire countryside have an atmosphere of caring that is very evident.

Canon Richard Askew, author of this chapter, works within Salisbury diocese, of which the Swanborough Team is a part. An Oxford graduate ordained in 1964, he is now Adviser on Mission and Ministry for the diocese as well as Treasurer of Salisbury Cathedral. He and his wife live with their four children in Salisbury itself. His interests are photography, sailing and travel.

A Beautiful Backdrop?

Wiltshire, like all the best sermons, is divided into three parts. To the south there lies a land of wind-swept uplands, dotted with red flags and warning notices and re-echoing with the crump of artillery shells; for this is Salisbury Plain, the army's private no-go area. The north-west runs out into sub-industrial squalor, all the more unattractive for its rural location. But the north-east of the county is prime agricultural land, best quality Middle England, where the beef barons and the corn kings purr contentedly along the muddy lanes in their Range Rovers. This part of Wiltshire has been described as 'a factory with the roof off', and certainly it gives the appearance of a model of neat husbandry: good land well used but not exploited. In this precious little green belt, nestling between the Plain to the south and the M4 and the 'western corridor' to the north, lie farms, green fields and thatched cottages that add up to every Englishman's ideal picture of the countryside.

It was in this rich and smiling landscape that the first summit conference in our national history took place. In 871 King Alfred met his brother Ethelred at Swanborough Tump, a modest roadside mound, and it was here that they settled the question of the inheritance should the Danes do anything regrettable to one or other of them in battle. The Tump had already become the meeting place for the peasant farmers of the Swanborough Hundred—a tract of country originally allotted to some hundred Saxon invaders as the fruits of their victory over the native Britons in the sixth century. A 'Hundred' court used to meet here up until the nineteenth century when, by common consent, the councillors decided to adjourn to the 'Rose & Crown' at Woodborough.

While today this delectable part of the country presents a strictly rural face, this is to some extent misleading. The railway which whisks you from Pewsey station to Paddington in under an hour means that the commuter belt actually extends even as far as this part of Wiltshire. While the numbers engaged in work on the land have inevitably declined with mechanisation, they have been replaced either by up-and-coming executives who like the idea of keeping one wellington boot in the country, or by retired people. The population is approximately what it was in 1880.

The Swanborough Team

Ecclesiastically, Swanborough is a necklace of little villages and hamlets, grouped into the Swanborough Team—eight villages together with nine church buildings. In population they range from tiny Huish (27 inhabitants) up to North Newnton, boasting 294 residents. The total population of the team is 2,100.

In former times, when the sun of Victorian affluence shone on the countryside, each of these churches denoted a separate parish, with its own incumbent and sprawling, impractical parsonage house. Today the team is the responsibility of a team rector, a team vicar and a team curate. While the rector and vicar have pastoral care for half the villages each, all three are used to moving around all the churches, contributing generally to the life of this close-knit team.

The present team rector of the Swanborough Team is the Rev John Whettem, a Cambridge graduate in his early sixties, who is also Rural Dean of the Pewsey Deanery. A cheerful, twinkling man, well-rounded in figure and personality, John presides over his 25 square miles with a style that is 'laid back', jovial and approachable. Before coming to Swanborough in 1980, his experience had been mainly urban—15 years in Bristol, including five as a youth chaplain; three in Wandsworth; and then 12 in a semi-rural situation near Chichester. 'We had three churches which you could call country; when I came here I realised that this was country and that wasn't.'

New Challenges

John Whettem's move to deep Wiltshire faced him with
three new situations: congregations were inevitably
smaller, in line with the population pattern of his hamlets;
resistance to change, particularly liturgical change, was
more marked; and, for the first time, he was working with
colleagues in a team. He has adapted to these three factors,
sensing the opportunities for deeper pastoral care and
spiritual growth offered by work with small groups by
establishing a basis of trust which has enabled him to satisfy
the aspirations both of the traditionalists and the progres-
sives within the pattern of services on offer; and by welding
together a close clergy team from men who do not necessarily come from his own theological stable. The clergy fellowship is maintained and developed by shared worship, Bible
study and prayer and a weekly shared meal for themselves
and their families. John himself is the product of an
evangelical college—Wycliffe Hall—but confesses to 'a
firm resistance in my own mind to belonging to any group.'
He does, however, describe himself as 'charismatic'.

   John took over the Swanborough Team as the third team
rector. The first two had had the difficult task of drawing together into a team an ever-increasing number of disparate,
and occasionally resentful, parishes and churches. In 1970
it started with four parishes and six churches. By 1980 it had
grown to eight parishes and ten churches. This amalgamation had been carried through with care and skill, so that
John was able to embark on a period of consolidation. He
has built up a pattern of consistency in the services, so that
every parish has one service a Sunday, except for the
monthly occasion when all join in team services. By guaran-
teeing traditional 1662 worship at certain points, he has
freed up other occasions for liturgical development and experiment. Choirs are no longer feasible as they were 15
years back, but this has been used as an opportunity to introduce freer patterns of worship music—*Mission Praise* is
now widely used. Traditional congregations now feel happy

to begin to engage in open intercessions during the Eucharist. Congregations always exceed 5% of the population and sometimes improve on 10%.

A More Caring Approach

John's first move, therefore, was to build up a pattern of services in which all could find nurture, provided they were prepared to travel round the team a little. For the most part, this they are willing to do. John and his two ordained colleagues have the assistance of two lay readers, together with the retired former team rector who lives locally and assists when he can. The coming church-to-be is catered for by a couple of Sunday schools within the team, each with a healthy 20 to 25 or so children, and a youth club for the teens. Apart from Sundays, there is a mid-week Communion service, celebrated in a house, and a Mothers' Union branch organised across the team.

This is not a community which requires large organisations to care for it: the contribution of the church lies mainly in individual acts of good neighbourliness. It is an area with few social problems apart from those occasioned by the affluent influx of commuters. Younger people often move away on getting married because they cannot cope with local house prices. There is the inevitable friction between the new commuters and the older village residents who doubt the newcomers' attachment to the community. However, all join in an appreciation of the church's role and in a commitment to preserving the church buildings. This, inevitably, can be a very heavy financial burden indeed. John has presided over the raising and spending of about £50,000 on maintaining the buildings over his seven years—a heavy millstone round his neck, but what else can one do but preserve such little gems as the Saxon church at Manningford Bruce, which is one of his responsibilities? This aspect of stewardship is perhaps reflected in the order of priorities revealed in the Swanborough Team 'Statement of Aims' posted up in each church porch—

Each parish is committed to three objects—

1 To work with love and care to maintain our parish church and its grounds in the beauty of holiness as the House of God.

2 To worship in such a way that our service will be inspiring and helpful to all.

3 To witness to the power of our faith in Christ by the purity of our daily life at home, at work and in the community.

Buildings or People?

Though buildings are a necessary responsibility, for John the real priority is people. Much growth has resulted from his mid-week 'Swanborough Fellowship', which gathers every Wednesday evening in the rectory. The pattern is varied, featuring, once a month, a guest speaker on some Christian topic and always including prayer and worship. It is preceded by a friendly picnic meal shared together in the comfort of John's home. So fruitful has this pattern proved that John has now encouraged the group, despite its reluctance, to move out into four separate home groups, which meet twice a month on their own, before coming back for the two other weeks to a joint meeting at the rectory.

Lay involvement is being carried further by the use of lay pastoral assistants—one already working and eight in training—to deepen and extend pastoral care. In terms of overall lay leadership, the eight parochial church councils are soon to be groomed for more independent responsibility, with lay chairmen to take over some of the regular responsibilities for the councils, at present carried by the clergy. The role of the central Team Council (two representatives from each parish) is being correspondingly strengthened.

How Do We Approach Mission?

What about all those aspects of looking outwards—all
grouped under the word 'mission'? The team made a big
effort at the time of Mission England, and despite the problems of transportation, was able to fill a coach to go to
Bristol—'It was a very good day and we were blessed by it.
Quite a few found new life—people already on the fringe
really, so it wasn't a question of picking them up. They've
just gone on and they have been built in'.

A delayed reaction to Mission England was the 'Festival
of Faith' which John set up across the whole deanery in
1985. This was a major effort involving all 24 churches of
the deanery in a ministry of teaching, exploring new areas
of Christian work and worship and enjoying one another's
fellowship. A teaching seminar led by the Rev John
Payton, a 'Parable' drama group from Oxford, a liturgical
dance group, a 'Prom Praise' concert and a Bible Society
presentation made up a full programme. The week culmi-
nated in a great shared eucharist which, under the theme of
'Christ Triumphant', brought together some 400
communicants.

Ecumenical possibilities are necessarily limited in an
area with no other denomination represented in significant
numbers. However, the team does relate to the Church overseas, both through the diocesan link with the Anglican
Church in the Sudan, and—more particularly—through
their special ties with the work of the South American
Missionary Society in Paraguay. Here Eileen Murphy, who
is adopted by Swanborough, serves as a teacher. The connection has been further cemented by two visits of Paraguayan
schoolchildren, a dozen at a time, to the team. These have
gone off very happily and have made the missionary connection a personal one for many parishioners.

A Healing Ministry

But the heart of John Whettem's ministry lies not so much in the occasional big event as in his deep, continuing ministry of healing and counselling. This in turn has stemmed from his own experience of renewal some 15 years ago. 'I was very, very dry as a parish priest, looking for new life in myself, and I received the baptism of the Spirit about 1971. That was a tremendous time of blessing for me, and from then I went on, and the healing ministry and the counselling work developed. I just became convinced of the goodness within it, and I think in a quiet way I have carried that on into the team.' It was his own healing from a debilitating stammer which brought John into the ministry of healing: 'I really couldn't get through a service or anything without getting absolutely stuck. I went to all sorts of people for help and it was only after the baptism of the Spirit that the thing just dissolved. It was one of the things that convinced me that, if *I* could be healed, then there wasn't much else that others couldn't be healed of.'

John's concern for healing is now expressed through healing services within the monthly pattern, and also informally as an individual ministry available at any time. He describes the basis of this work as follows—'The expectation I give to people is that you cannot come to God without being blessed'. He sees the main difficulty in the ministry of healing precisely in this question of the expectations people bring: 'When you get carried away with the idea that Jesus heals, you expect everybody to be healed instantly—and when they aren't, depression sets in a bit. You think, "Oh well this doesn't work" or "This isn't right", or even worse than that, "I am giving people false hope and I mustn't do it, so I must stop." Thank God we've got beyond that point.' John sees his counselling ministry as an integral part of his healing ministry: 'In the counselling the greatest healings we have are on the emotional side. This is very real and very good, and so that has been my main work. That's where I see the blessing. But on the physical side, not so great, although very real.'

John shares his counselling work with his wife, Mary, and Thursday afternoons are set aside for this purpose. Their 'client' for the week joins them for lunch and then a three-hour session concludes with a cup of tea. Their counselling approach derives from a form of ministry called 'Wholeness Through Christ'—John describes it as 'deep counselling with prayer, relying on the gifts of the Spirit and the exercise of them during the counselling'.

A Quiet and Gentle Impact

Viewed initially by his parishioners as 'a little bit askance at times, as if we are slightly mad' there has now grown up a deep respect within the church for the healing ministry which he inherited and has developed. Those who have found genuine blessing have passed the word around and a very different atmosphere now surrounds this aspect of ministry.

In his seven years as team rector, John has initiated gentle change while consolidating the team as a caring reality. His sensitive treatment both of small congregations and his mid-week fellowship have produced growth, both in numbers and in Christian maturity. But, above all in quiet and personal ways, here is a Christ-centred ministry that goes deep. An Argos poster in the rectory hall bears the caption 'Most miracles come quietly': it could serve as a comment on the work of the Swanborough Team.

Chapter 8

Bryn Moriah Pentecostal Church, Cynwyl Elfed, Dyfed

Barry Osborne

*'Real commitment and public witness ... a
burden to pray for the local young people'*

*In a tiny Welsh village with a name that reminds one of the
names in Tolkien's* Lord of the Rings *stories, the Spirit of
God has moved quite dramatically. Where chapels were
closing and spiritual paralysis was the order of the day, Bryn
Moriah was coming to life. Young people in particular met
with God, and Barry Osborne describes in detail how their
own and others' lives changed as a result. Visitation teams of
young people formed, and those who had never heard or
who had forgotten the Gospel entered into a fresh faith.
Reading this chapter, we meet a gallery of ordinary people
whom God has transformed.*

*Barry Osborne is Secretary/Treasurer of the Federation for
Rural Evangelism and has been active in rural evangelism
through Mission for Christ since 1963. He is general secretary of this society and a member of the inter-denominational
team ministry working with village churches nationwide.
Barry is married with a foster son and says that his hobby is
business management!*

The village of Cynwyl Elfed is a small dot on the map along
the A484 road north from Carmarthen. No more than 150

people live in the village, although over twice as many live in the farming area around the village, which boasts one garage, one shop, one pub, one cobbler's workshop (shoe mender), a primary school and two places of worship. Scattered around the village there are isolated houses, clusters of cottages and a few more chapels here and there.

A Dramatic Start

Our story begins in one of these, a Congregational chapel where shortly after the 1904 Welsh Revival the Sunday school Bible class was discussing 'assurance of salvation'. Much to the amazement of the rest of the class, a young girl named Rachel Jones testified to having received such an assurance. Her testimony provoked a harsh reaction from all but one of the Sunday school teachers, who alone sided with Rachel.

Strangely, that evening at the chapel service the Sunday school teacher, Mr Osborne Davies, was convicted that he had lied about his own salvation and cried to God to forgive him. Immediately he was soundly converted and the Holy Spirit gave him the same assurance that Rachel enjoyed.

Persecution!

The impact of both testimonies was considerable, and many other members of the chapel also were saved. However, persecution quickly followed, and those who had become part of the revival movement were forced to leave. They met regularly in a local farmhouse and continued to pray for those members remaining at the Congregational chapel who until then had not shared in this experience. God continued to bless them, and their numbers increased daily.

By 1912 a new chapel had been built, about 6 miles from the centre of the village and ¼ mile from the Congregational chapel. It was called Bryn Moriah, and the special opening services were conducted by the Rev R B Jones from Porth, in the Rhondda valley. Services were conducted in Welsh, and the chapel remained independent.

The fellowship remained stable until the 1930s, when it went into sharp decline. Many members moved away from the area. Others were called into the forces. The life of the chapel reached a low ebb, which coincided with the cessation of the prayer meetings. Tragically, by the mid 1940s only a tiny handful of people met at Bryn Moriah, and the future looked bleak.

During the late 1940s the work picked up a little, mainly as a result of the work of a Mr Trefor Dakin, an Elim minister who travelled from Tumble, a village over 20 miles to the south-east of Cynwyl. Mr Dakin commenced an annual series of evangelistic meetings, conducted two meetings each month, and officiated at weddings and funerals.

The Promise of Blessing

The next significant development was at the end of the 1960s when, through the gifts of the Spirit, the Lord revealed that he was going to call people of a different tongue to the fellowship and to increase the congregation. The membership at this time was about 10 adults with a small Sunday school.

Not long afterwards, several English-speaking people moved into the area. A few were already committed Christians, and they attached themselves to the church despite the language barrier. Other English-speaking people were converted and also joined the church. The prophecy was being fulfilled. At the same time, a number of young people who had been brought up in Bryn Moriah were converted as a result of various influences. It was a real wave of blessing.

In 1979 the pastor and elders agreed that the Sunday morning service would be in English. Normally this would be quite a traumatic issue for those whose native language is Welsh, but God's hand was undeniably at work in their midst, and although some of the older members found the change difficult they happily followed where he led. By 1984 the little chapel, which seats about 80, was filled mostly with English-speaking people.

More recently there has been significant development with some of the youth in the fellowship. Towards the end of 1984 God laid a burden to pray for the local young people on the hearts of some of the members. By the May of 1985 14 young people—mostly teenagers—had been converted. Some of these came under conviction of sin and were saved in their own homes as they prayed for forgiveness. All were very zealous and eager to share their faith with others.

The First was Sian

The first to make a response was Sian, a young girl who had come to the area from Carmarthen to train in agriculture. The farmer's wife, Carol Jones, is a Sunday school teacher at Bryn Moriah, but when Sian first moved in with Carol and her family on the farm she carefully distanced herself from anything Christian. Finally she was persuaded to attend a meeting where a group called 'Sound Decision' was singing.

The group was originally formed around seven daughters of one of the members, who was a niece of Mr Osborne Davies (one of the founders of Bryn Moriah). Over several years the group had sung at various special events, and their ministry had been the means of bringing a number of people in the area into faith in Christ.

Sian was moved by the singing and started to attend Bryn Moriah regularly. Noticing the change in her life, Carol asked her if she had accepted Jesus Christ as her Saviour, and received and enthusiastic response of 'Oh, yes!' So it was that another phase of conversions began.

Not Long Afterwards Came Neil

Already several of the members of the church felt a deep urge to pray for the conversion of a boy called Neil. Neil was a local lad but was away from home attending college at Cardiff, studying biochemistry. Despite growing up in the local Methodist chapel where he had particularly enjoyed Sunday school, Neil was glad to have escaped from the strong Christian influence of his childhood. But attempts to find satisfaction in the world were disappointing.

It was during his second year at college that events took a surprising turn. He had made friends with another boy at college called Ian, but was surprised to find that college life was not the only thing they had in common. For Ian, too, was escaping from a Christian background. After talking about the emptiness they both felt, the two boys decided to attend an evangelical church in the city where they found to their surprise that they quite enjoyed the services. Not long afterwards Ian made a response at one of these services. The change hit Neil like a bombshell.

Two months later Neil was back home in the village and decided to call on Dai Rees, whose home he had visited many times before. Dai, his wife and three daughters live in the middle of Cynwyl Elfed, and their home is a centre for fellowship for young people. Five years earlier when Neil had first visited the Rees family, Dai had challenged him with the gospel, emphasising the personal nature of salvation and the experience of assurance of salvation.

Although Neil had consistently rejected their testimony, he could not ignore the family's obvious sincerity. Now his footsteps returned, and as Dai talked with him he gradually realised the inadequacy of his self-righteousness and how much he needed Christ. It was well after midnight when Neil left that home with Dai's words ringing in his ears. 'You know what to do. Now go home and do it.'

Back home Neil began to pray and asked the Lord to come into his life, but nothing seemed to happen. The story is best told in his own words.

'By 2.45 am I felt no better, so I turned to my Bible for

help. It fell open at Acts chapter 2 and my attention was drawn to verse 21 where I read '... everyone who calls on the name of the Lord will be saved.' Here was my answer! He had *promised* to answer, and I knew that I had to thank him for all he had done for me, coming down from glory and dying on the cross. As I prayed again it was with real gratitude for all he had done. Such peace and joy flooded my heart that I wanted to wake up the whole village to tell them about it!'

Visitation Evangelism in Reverse!

About the same time that Neil made his commitment, God was at work through another member of the church— Carol's mother, Mrs Peggy Edwards. A lady who had moved into the village in the autumn of 1984 was selling kitchen appliances from house to house. Her name was Mrs Linda Cook, and when she called at Peggy's home, she was invited in and offered a cup of tea. Soon they were chatting but not about kitchen appliances! As together they talked about the Bible, Linda felt that she would like to accompany Peggy to a service at Bryn Moriah.

The first thing that Linda noticed when she arrived at the chapel was the sense of the presence of God and the reality of the faith of those who worshipped there. Never before had she been to a service where so many of the congregation shared publicly in the worship. She continued to attend regularly, taking her teenage daughter, Samantha, who was also affected by the sense of God's presence and the style of worship. First Linda received Christ as her personal Saviour in her own home. Not long after her daughter followed in her steps.

Several members of the church were actively involved in Mission Wales and videos of the Billy Graham meetings were being shown in the area. Dai Rees and his family took the Cooks, and at the close of the meeting Samantha made her public response and was counselled by one of Dai's daughters.

Real commitment and public witness seem to be signifi-

cant aspects of the church life at Bryn Moriah, and
Samantha is active in her school Christian Union. That
summer Samantha's brother visited for a holiday and Linda
experienced the joy of leading her own son to know the
Saviour—an experience she describes as an 'enormous
privilege'.

God was Using Different Members

The way in which God was using different members of the
church in personal evangelism throughout this period
stands out clearly to an observer. A young man called Emyr
started work as an apprentice bricklayer in the autumn of
1984. His boss, Mr Hywel Slaymaker, is the youth leader at
Bryn Moriah, and not long afterwards Hywel and his wife
took Emyr with them to one of the Saturday night youth
meetings. Emyr was amazed to see so many young people
at the meeting and quickly noticed their love for one
another. It was a different world from his usual life of pubs
and discos.

Life has been particularly hard on Emyr, and in the
March of 1985 he was feeling particularly low when his boss
invited him home for a cup of tea. But Emyr found more
than a cup of tea that evening, for a missionary staying in
the home shared his faith and gave Emyr a tract. He knew
he needed to be saved and prayed earnestly for two weeks.
Then one day he knew God had answered. All the hurt inside had been healed; a far deeper satisfaction was found in
Jesus.

Emyr's public confession came at one of the Billy
Graham videos at Newcastle Emlyn. Here too Sian's
brother, Alan, who had been another of the subjects of
prayer in the church, committed his life to Christ.

Mobilising the Sunday School

The church operates an all-age Sunday school. The senior Bible class meets in the vestry and is taught in Welsh. Several classes have to share the use of the chapel, but in order to accommodate the senior English-speaking class a caravan had been placed next to the chapel. Willing workers had stripped out the inside and fixed seating around the walls. Here Carol Jones the farmer's wife leads a class of about 24 teenager and adults. Many of the new converts were part of this class.

During the monthly youth rally in January 1986 Carol received a compelling burden to lead the young people in taking the gospel out among the people in the area, but a sense of inadequacy held her back until her sister-in-law told her that the youth leader in a church in Carmarthen also had received such a burden at about the same time. Encouraged by their common vision they arranged to venture out with young people from both churches working together.

The first outreach was on 19th April, 1986. Meanwhile Carol turned the weekly Sunday school lesson into a training class for faith sharing. For several months she prepared the members of the senior Sunday school class by making them think through the answers to awkward questions they may be asked. The idea worked well and made the group study the Scriptures more for themselves.

The First Attempt

Carol and her group were glad to be able to team up with the young people from Carmarthen, where a strong work was established. The Carmarthen youth leader had adapted a questionnaire as an aid to evangelism, and because of the significant numbers of Welsh-speaking people in the area the questionnaire had also been specially translated. The Welsh culture is strong, and it was important that the team could evangelise in Welsh. But it was the fact that the young people were well known in the small community that caused the greatest impact.

When the day finally came it was with great trepidation that a group of 24 (some from Bryn Moriah and some from the church in Carmarthen) set out on their first attempt at door-to-door evangelism. They had decided on a visit to the village where Emyr lived.

As they huddled into the bus shelter for a quick prayer meeting, Neil was deeply conscious of the challenge of witnessing to people where they were well known. He realised that they could not afford to make mistakes and wondered how he would manage if he called on a very devout person who knew his Bible better than he did! He was not alone with his fears, but all realised that God could be relied on to help them. Finally they set out.

Later that day they talked together excitedly about their experiences. Many people had listened eagerly, and most of the 24 were willing to do it again.

Going Solo and Being Faithful

Those who had come from Carmarthen could only go visiting on Saturdays, but after several weeks Carol and the others from Bryn Moriah wanted to go out on Wednesday evenings, too. The problem was that this would generate extra costs for tracts and materials, and Carol wondered whether they could afford it.

The next day one of the older members at Bryn Moriah approached Carol with a gift of £50.00 to be used for the outreach work. 'You mean it's for the youth leader in Carmarthen?' she asked. 'No,' she was told, 'it's for your work.' Carol could hardly believe it. She had not even begun to pray, and the need was met!

Not all those who have tried this ministry have felt that this is something they should do again, but there is a nucleus of about a dozen. Sometimes even *their* enthusiasm wanes. One Wednesday evening Emyr felt far from zealous, but another Christian boy called Chris encouraged him. After prayer they set out and visited one of the local farms where a teenage girl listened attentively. Her face lit up as she realised that Jesus Christ has died for her. Shortly after she moved away from the area but has continued to go on in the faith.

God Can Overrule

On another occasion plans had been made to visit surrounding farms but only four people turned up with one car between them. Obviously there would have to be a change of plans. After prayer they felt that they should visit one particular area. As they set out it started to pour with rain but stopped briefly as they arrived at their destination.

Carol and Neil set off in one direction while Alan and Jackie went elsewhere. Jackie's family had moved into the area the previous year from Manchester. As they reached the first two houses it began to rain again. Finding no response, Alan and Jackie returned to the car. Meanwhile Carol and Neil had found a local man from another denomination in his garage so while the rain kept falling they kept talking. (One of the most interesting aspects of the visitation work is the number of professing Christians from other churches that the visitors meet. Sometimes they have little understanding of the gospel, and the visits result in a revival of faith.)

Forty-five minutes later as the rain stopped, Neil and Carol went back to find the others, anxious to share with them how they had found an extraordinary liberty in witnessing and that the gentleman had shown a deep interest. However, they found Jackie and Alan had their own story. As they had returned to the car they soon realised that Carol and Neil must have made a 'successful' contact and so began to pray for them. As they had begun to pray they were both made aware of God's presence with them in the car and for forty-five minutes had been lost in praise and prayer.

The importance of God's guidance and help in their visits is paramount in the work. Even when the situations seem hopeless, God can overrule. Once a Sunday school teacher who was visited confessed that spiritually he was in the dark. He drank in everything he was told by his visitors, and as they rose to leave, the man's wife grasped the literature they offered, as a starving person grasps proffered food.

The visitation team has also become aware of the sovereignty of God in the work of spreading the gospel. They see themselves as seed sowers and leave the harvest to God. Occasionally they are rebuffed, but about 45% of the people visited welcome them, most inviting them into their homes and giving them refreshment while they witness.

One of the saddest contacts Carol recalls is a young man who told her that when he was a boy he had nearly accepted Jesus Christ as his Saviour but was discouraged by his friends. With tears coursing down his face he said, 'I know you are telling me the truth, but I don't want to lose my friends'.

'We force no one,' said Carol, remembering the occasion some time later. 'There are many like him. We can only pray and wait, expecting God to work.'

As she told me of her experiences it was obvious that Carol was aware that not all were called to this kind of evangelism. It was also clear that God was using many different channels. The regular services at Bryn Moriah have played an important part, particularly the prayer-life of the fellowship and the encouragement of the pastor and other church leaders. The special monthly youth meetings at Bryn Moriah and the fellowship and co-operation of the Christians in Carmarthen—even the informal fellowship provided by Christian homes in the area—all have played their part.

The visitation programme has been most effective among two groups of people. Some have developed a folk religion based on good works. There is often a lack of knowledge of the Scriptures and consequently, prior to the visits, many understood nothing of the issues of redemption. The belief that chapel-going and good works guarantee salvation is a common misunderstanding.

Another group is formed by those who have grown up with a knowledge of the gospel but who have not realised its power in their lives. It is in this group that the message of assurance of salvation—which originally brought the work of Bryn Moriah into being—is still bringing joy and peace through believing.

A Growing Vision

However, some would claim that the group that has benefited most is the young Christians themselves. As they have engaged in a regular programme of evangelism, it has added a vital quality to their Christian life. Growth in the individual Christians' lives has in turn benefited the whole church.

Throughout the period of growth there have been changes, but these have generally gone smoothly. Indeed, very few people have left Bryn Moriah. Two families who were attending from a nearby village felt called to establish an evangelical witness in Pencader. Initially meetings were held in the village hall, but now the congregation has moved into part of an existing chapel building. Two other families and one lady also felt called to support their local Church in Wales in Velindre, Llandyssul, and also went out with the blessing of the church.

Much of the growth of the church is due to the good leadership of Pastor Dewi Davies, who joined the church as a member in 1957 and was appointed pastor in 1962. Pastor Davies gives the main factors for growth as fervent prayer and the clear presentation of the gospel. The Sunday morning congregation just about fills the chapel and of the 80 or so who attend, about half live very locally. The Sunday evening congregation is smaller partly because of the isolated situation of the chapel and partly because the service is conducted in Welsh. In the week there are special revival prayer meetings each Monday in addition to the regular prayer and Bible study meeting each Thursday.

The congregation now plans to build a new and larger

chapel building adjacent to the existing one, which will then be used for smaller meetings. All the finances are being generated through prayer and the giving of the members, without any special fund-raising activities.

Two or three of the young men from Bryn Moriah became concerned about the many young people who attended the discos and pubs in Carmarthen on Saturday evenings. Some of these were friends they have grown up with. In the autumn of 1986 they began street evangelism, reaching them as they left the pubs and discos late at night.

They established a pattern of meeting up with other local Christians and praying for an hour. At 11.00 pm they go out and are often actively witnessing until midnight or even later. They get a mixed reception.

God is also leading several young women in the fellowship into missionary service. They are travelling widely both in Britain and abroad, so God's Word is going out from a church in a small rural community in Wales.

Here then is a village church with a vision for evangelism and with prayer as a priority. Life in a small village church is often vexed by problems that assume disproportionate dimensions. Bryn Moriah stands as a testimony to the value of lifting our eyes from ourselves and our problems and fixing them instead on the needs of those around who know not Christ, and most importantly of all, keeping them fixed on Christ himself.

Chapter 9

St Patrick's, Bampton with Mardale, Cumbria

John Berry

'You can't shear sheep in a hurry and do a good job of it'

The parish of Bampton in Cumbria is set in some of England's most breath-taking scenery. The main occupation in the area is hill-farming, a job as old as the hills in which the village nestles. A romantic vision of rural bliss is coupled with some of the more brutal aspects of life in Bampton: sheep being buried in the snow; children travelling miles to school; the Chernobyl disaster preventing farmers from selling lambs at the height of the season. Through difficult times, St Patrick's church stands firm, a symbol of security and stability. Things change slowly in Bampton, but changing they are.

Rev John Berry, who was the minister for St Patrick's until 1986, gives us a vivid picture of Bampton life in this chapter. Through entertaining anecdotes and poignant glimpses of sadder times, we are drawn into the atmosphere of this rural parish. John, his wife Jennifer, and their three children, moved from an inner-city parish to the Lake District. John has now left Cumbria to lead a team of Anglican churches near Chesterfield in Derbyshire. His favourite uses of spare time are reading and ornithology.

I was sitting behind a rather shaky whist table in a small
vestry. The church was right out in rural Cumbria, and I
had driven, it seemed, miles through the fields to get to it.
There was a smell of damp in the air, the constant sound of
lambs bleating which made concentration difficult, and the
wind whistled through the cracks around the door. The
PCC huddled before an electric fire, leaving the vicar and
myself shivering in the cold. Eight faithful people looked
rather suspiciously at me as I was jokingly introduced as
'The Bishop's Evangelism Man, sent to sort out trouble-
some parishes'.

Only a few weeks before I had moved with my family
from a flourishing city-centre parish where we had seen
many happy times. We had introduced several new things
successfully, and the modern family services, lunchtime
meetings for shoppers, coffee mornings, house groups, a
soup-run for vagrants, and the like had all brought new life
and vitality to the church. I had a great deal to share with
these folks in Cumbria.

My talk began with a biblical definition of evangelism,
followed by an array of illustrations of evangelistic events
from my own experience, mainly the ones which had shown
some success, and then I challenged them to reach out
themselves to the people of their community, particularly
the youngsters.

The audience sat rather stoically through my address
until I invited questions and discussion. An elderly farmer
smiled kindly at me and said: 'Young man—look out of that
there window. You see them hills? They haven't changed in
a thousand years. You don't expect us to change our ways
by hay-time do you?'

I Was in the Country, and I had a Lot of Learning to Do

School Begins

It all began with a Partners in Mission Consultation in the
diocese of Carlisle, at which the Bishop of Madras in

particular had drawn attention to the lack of personal sharing of the faith amongst church people, almost a reticence
about speaking the name of Jesus. This challenge, plus the
message of the Nationwide Initiative in Evangelism, led the
diocese to advertise for an Officer for Evangelism. Thus I
found myself moving to a very pretty village in the Lakes,
the parish of Bampton with Mardale, with its lovely little
church, a population of around 350, a village school with a
new keen headmaster, and a small but lively congregation.
Each week was to be divided between this parish (two
days), the diocese (four days), and my family and dog (one
day). In the diocese, my task was to initiate, train for and
assist in evangelism through the local churches. Just fancy,
driving round the Lakes, and being paid to do it. Kirkstone
Pass at 11.00 pm on a summer's evening is a wonderful experience. Heaton Cooper's paintings are no exaggeration,
I can tell you, for I've seen them all in real life. Of course,
I bought and read every book and paper on rural ministry I
could lay my hands on—not that there was a great deal. I
didn't find George Herbert's *The Country Parson* or
William Addison's *The English Country Parson* much help,
though highly entertaining. Then I discovered the writings
of Dr Anthony J Russell, particularly his booklet *The Village, Myth and Reality*. Here was what I needed. But still
not very much on evangelism.

Since those days, there has been a steady increase in research and writing on country matters. *Partners* magazine,
papers from the Rural Theology Association, Leslie
Francis' *Rural Anglicanism*, some very good material from
the Methodist Home Missions Department and the Church
of Scotland, the Channel 4 booklet *Country Crisis: The lid
off the chocolate box* and Canon John Poulton's *Fresh Air*
have all been very helpful.

But ... School is Where You are Learning

Yes. It was out in the parish, talking to people, caring for
them in their everyday needs, visiting country clergy and

church councils, getting involved in parish assessments,
that the real learning began to take place. And I made some
awful mistakes, bringing my urban assumptions and pre-
conceptions to bear on the problems, rather than starting
from where I was, in the country.

The Crisis in the Country

In many ways, what the books had warned me about was
true. The country was not what my urban romantic attitude
had taught me to think it was. For me, it had been a place
of relaxation and holidays, wandering down lanes, picking
wild flowers, scratching the neck of a horse over a fence,
laughing at lambs playing in the fields. Life seemed to move
at a very easy pace, there was always time for a 'crack' over
the farmyard gate, a pipe of 'baccy', or a can of tea and a
cheese sandwich on a bale of straw. Even the cattle-market
appeared to be a place for relaxation with a pint of ale for
most farmers.

Of course, I did experience and enjoy this side of country
life. It was extremely pleasant to take the dog outside the
gate and immediately be by a river where the salmon leapt,
the yellow wagtails swooped, and the dipper dipped; to
look up and see a pair of golden eagles or a buzzard or
peregrine falcon on the wing; not to have to lock my car up;
clean air, a good crop of raspberries, very friendly and helpful neighbours. It was heaven.

But I discovered another side to country life. The village
shop closed while we were in Bampton, and we had to rely
on vans, or drive nine miles to Penrith for shopping. The
village school was constantly under threat of closure as the
numbers fell below 25. Our children had to travel each day
to Penrith to secondary school, and if they forgot something it was an 18 mile round trip to take it to them. One
winter fortnight I kept count of the mileage I travelled taking my children in and out of Penrith for various things—it
had cost me over £50 in petrol. Apart from the works bus
each day, the only public transport was on market days.

There were not enough children to get any uniformed organisation off the ground; the village sports day (once famous throughout the Lakes) was becoming less and less viable.

Life was hard on the farm. While we were in Bampton, the snow cut off the village several times, bringing power lines down. Water pipes froze up. The river regularly overflowed its banks, cutting off one half of the village from the other. This was bad enough for us, but for the sheep and their owners it could be disaster. To have to dig down in the the deep drifts of snow for lost sheep, after walking through the snow and ice way up the fells, was no laughing matter. To wake up in the morning and find the whole valley flooded and hundreds of sheep drowned was heart-breaking. And then a lovely dry hot summer which pleased the tourists could leave the sheep with no grass to eat. And, of course, those tourists would bring dogs and leave gates open.

There are many tensions in rural life. Politics, unfortunately, comes into it, with decisions about quantity and quality of produce, subsidies and movement of stock all affecting planning of farm strategy. Should I sell my cottage that I no longer need, or my old barn, to a local person, or to a Londoner for a holiday home, and get three times the price? Should we keep our village with its 'oldie-worldie' appearance to attract the tourist, or modernise it to make living more comfortable for ourselves? Should we bring in some light industries to provide employment—oh, the Tourist Board won't allow that—or let our valley pastures be used for caravan sites instead of for sheep? While the country dweller tries to keep going, doing the work that his fathers and grandfathers did before him—the only thing he has really been trained to do—he finds the countryside is changing around him, and he can't do much about it. I began to learn very quickly that heart attacks, mental illness, alcoholism, even suicide, were not unknown in a village. And when something so far away as the Chernobyl disaster stops you selling your lambs at the best time, it seems as if life is just not worth it.

The Rural Church in Crisis

Perhaps because of all this change and tension, country folk often look to the church as the one place where they can count on things staying the same. To sit in church and hear the readings and liturgy that they heard as a child and to sing the old hymns makes them feel better—perhaps there is some hope after all.

This attitude in itself brings tension. It was often thought that the country parish is where the church put a clergyman who has worked hard and now needs a rest period, a man in the last few years of his ministry, or one with heart trouble. But with the amalgamation of rural parishes, groups and teams, ministry in the country means a lot of dashing around, covering a good many miles. In Cumbria we have seen a significant increase in young men coming to work in the rural areas, in both Anglican and Methodist churches. These men come with new ideas, wanting to introduce new songs, a music group, to have regular prayer meetings or fellowship times in the vicarage. Because they are young they are perhaps more in touch with the young, and they feel that if the latter are going to be attracted to church, then things must change. Also, into rural areas have moved people who have been brought up as Christians in lively city churches and do not want to—in their mind—take a step backwards. Others have young families and are concerned about them.

I have made my own mistakes in this area. I found that both church and chapel Sunday school annual outings always went to Morecambe. I suggested that we went a-cross to Bamburgh for a change. 'Why?' people asked. 'Are there shops there?' I got my own way and we went to Bamburgh. But a lot of those who would normally have come didn't. And the next year we didn't have an outing. I got upset over confirmation candidates who never came to church. I was inclined not to accept them for confirmation, but when I visited their homes discovered that to say I wasn't willing to present them for confirmation was interpreted as my saying that I didn't feel they had reached puberty yet; they had not grown up enough. This was an insult to the family. Confirmation was seen as more of an entrance into adulthood than into membership of the church. In fact, once a boy was confirmed he would, in many cases, cease to come to church, for Sunday worship was seen as a duty of women and children. Not that the men lacked a belief in God, but that in the order of things, the women represented the family in church.

These things can cause a lot of upset for both pastor and people. In a city, if a pastor does something you don't like you can move to another church. But in the country, this may not be so easy, so you simply stay away until that pastor has moved on to another church. And the ripples spread, for as I quickly discovered most of my parishioners were inter-related, and as one farmer succinctly put it, 'If you kick one, they all scream'.

I was certainly in school, having to listen and listen and listen again. Why did people react as they did? Was it for a good reason, that perhaps city life had dulled my mind to, and which needed encouraging and building on? Or was it something that had to be changed if the Kingdom was to grow? Not easy questions, but if tackled with a sense of adventure and with a growing love for the people, they turned out to be great fun.

A Course in Rural Ministry

What did I learn in this school?

I learned that most of my parishioners had a faith in God, but that it didn't always show up in Sunday attendance at church. Our local Methodist chapel had a very small membership, but on Anniversary Sunday it was packed with people. Christmas, Easter and Harvest services were well attended. Special services saw people standing round the sides, and the collection at a funeral could be in the order of £150–£200. When our church roof needed repairs, we raised several thousand pounds in the village. 'It's our church' they said.

Once or twice a year we would hold a Boon-Night, when the men would gather to give their time and efforts to the church, scything grass, repairing stone walls and straightening gravestones, after which the vicar had to take them to the pub for a drink. And when we purchased a new piece of ground for our churchyard, the stonewalling was done free of charge, and with great pride. Most families contributed to the envelope scheme. They were part of the church in that sense.

I learned that I had to love people for what they were, and not be too impatient to make them what my urban evangelical upbringing had led me to believe they should be. To go gently, for they were a gentle people. To share sincerely in their joys and sadnesses. To 'muck in' with them when another pair of hands was needed. Perhaps some of my greatest times of evangelism were when I sat in the dirty straw of a byre while the favourite cow of the farmer's wife slowly died; or when I was labouring for the men while they built a wall; helping in a most clumsy way to rescue sheep from the floods; standing at a graveside with a man who had just seen his life-partner buried and was now desolate; leaning over a farmyard gate; in the bar of the pub after a funeral; by a fireside miles up the fells in a lonely cottage—that was when God could be talked about naturally and without embarrassment.

I think I learned to use opportunities as they arose, to accept people's offerings to God, whatever they were, whether they be at worship in church or cutting grass. To be oneself and not pretend to be better than they, and to love people into the Kingdom of God. I wish I had learned some of these lessons earlier in my ministry. It took the village of Bampton to teach me.

There was a great temptation to sink into this patient pastoring of people and gradually lose all expectancy. This I noticed in too many of my fellow rural clergy, that they had an extremely low level of expectancy in their ministry, and evangelism frightened them.

I was aware of the children and young people in the villages, and their needs. They were using computers in schools, a sign of the rapid change that was coming about in their lifetime. They must see that the Good News of Christ is as relevant today as it was for their grandfathers in their day. What was the church saying to this new generation?

With the limited time we had in the village, I felt that this was where we would put out resources—into a work amongst young people. We were fortunate in having a committed Christian headmaster (wife and family) at our village school. He allowed me to go into school each week and to take assemblies and teach RE. Of course, this could not be in any way evangelistic. But it meant I got to know the children well, and could integrate my teaching on Sundays with that I gave them in school. Then, with the chapel, we set up a Good News Club for this same age group, for an hour or so after school. Our Sunday school was altered slightly in its timing so that the children came in to church before the Peace. I would preach on the same passage of Scripture that they studied in Sunday school, and they would be invited to share some aspect of that with the rest of the congregation—a poem, a song, some drama or pictures, which made them feel a part of the worshipping family.

We then redecorated our attic for the teenagers to use as a meeting place. Once a week they could study together from the *Serendipity* workbooks. Every opportunity was taken to get them out of their own surroundings to meet with other Christians of their own age.

I think our aim became one of gently showing the love of Christ, and gradually teaching the truths of the Christian gospel in the context of village life, so that these marvellous Cumbrian folks might fall in love with the Risen Christ. And when this happened, and one of these gentle people began to serve Christ daily, he became a force to be reckoned with.

Taking the Lessons Learned in School out to Others who were Struggling

As I travelled around Cumbria I found several clergy and church councils struggling with falling numbers, elderly congregations, financial problems and the like. Simply to talk to them about evangelism tended to make them feel guilty rather than encourage them. I had to somehow find a way to help them see the possibilities that were there and use them with expectancy and hope. Rather than lecture to them, I found myself more and more visiting a parish for several days, to chat with the people within and outside the worshipping congregation. This was to make an assessment of where the church was, what resources the members had at their disposal, and what action they could take in the immediate and long-term future. My greatest joy was to see their faces light up in anticipation, to hear them say, 'Yes, we could do that. When do we start?'—to leave a meeting almost unnoticed because they were too busy planning to say goodbye to me.

But let's return to Bampton and observe two very different projects which, to me, could both be classed as evangelistic:

The Village Mission, and Results

I had only been in the village for about a year when information began to flow into my letter box from Mission England. Of course, the main part was to organise parties to go and hear Dr Billy Graham at Liverpool or Sunderland. But many of our villagers had hardly ever strayed away from their immediate surroundings. Lancaster was almost 'foreign', let alone Liverpool. But we tried, and did get a number to go across to Sunderland. Part way through the meeting I noticed one of our farmer's wives with tears in her eyes. Oh dear, I thought, the meeting has upset her. But when I asked her why she cried she replied: 'It suddenly struck me what a big family I belong to. All these Christians singing to God.' And this is one of the problems of evangelism in a small village. People very seldom get the opportunity to meet with large numbers of Christians. They are tempted to feel that the church is that Sunday gathering of perhaps 20 folk in the village church. The large meeting can give the village Christian a new understanding, a new vision and a new confidence.

But I wasn't satisfied with a coach to Sunderland. Some of us had prayed together about how to use the national initiative to bring the Good News to the centre of village life. The result was initially a ten-day period of mission in the villages and market towns of Cumbria and North Lancashire. We chose February when the farmers would not be so busy. Teams were invited from many theological and Bible colleges. To Bampton came a team of six students from Capernwray Bible School, led by an Anglican deaconess, Pamela Hamilton.

We spent quite some time with the student team preparing them. Only one had his home in England. The others came from the USA, Germany and Northern Ireland. None had worked in a village situation. So it was vital that they understand the kind of life and people that they were coming to live with. Some were housed in villagers' homes while others lived in a holiday cottage. The latter proved very useful for the students could invite people, especially teenagers, back for coffee and a chat to the cottage. These chats often continued into the early hours of the morning.

The main emphasis of the mission was the joy of the Christian life. So our main weeknight meetings were funnights, with games, lots to eat, sketches by the students and a short epilogue. Over a hundred people came to these evenings. During the day the team visited homes, spoke at coffee parties, and taught in school. They also ran a Good News club after school for all the youngsters who wished to stay on. Sundays, of course, the team spent in the church and chapel, assisting in worship.

Not everything was successful. The teaching in the school

was almost a disaster because some of the parents thought
the students were brainwashing their children in school
time. We had a most successful film evening, showing
Tanglewoods Secret, so we tried another—but this time
only five turned up. However, there was certainly success.
The witness of the students to the teenagers, plus a visit to
Kendal to hear Eric Delve, produced a lively Attic Club.
The impact on adults was less obvious at first. Only later
when the church held a stewardship mission did we realise
how much the mission had meant to so many of the adults,
in the way they responded in their giving and supporting.

Two other results are worth mentioning: an area Bible
study and prayer group, linking Christians from several villages for regular fellowship; and a continuing link with
Capernwray Bible School.

The Anniversary of the Church: 850 Years

One of the good things about the mission was that we had
encouraged the traditional village attitude of involvement.
The Women's Institute had made the food for one of the
fun evenings, for instance. This became a major part of our
intentions in celebrating the 850th anniversary of our
church. How could we best get every member of the community involved in something which spoke of the Good
News of Christ down the ages?

The result of our thinking was a weekend of celebration,
giving thanks for the faithfulness of God: exhibitions in the
church and village halls, illustrating past and present life in
church and community; all the school children involved in
a pageant, and as many of the local craftspeople and artists
who were willing to be involved showing off their wares and
selling them.

The weekend provided so many opportunities for witness and working together. I shall never forget one man
who had been quite anti the church coming to me to suggest
future ways the village could come together and help the
church communicate its message.

The same year proved also to be the 50th anniversary of the damming of the valley of Mardale to produce the Haweswater Reservoir. So, once again, we got together to organise an open-air service by the dam wall.

All of this showed me the importance in the village of history, the extended family, community involvement and the like, and the fact that the church was leading the encouragement of these things was a parable of the Good News in Christ.

Sheepshearing

In my five and a half years in rural Cumbria I never found myself thinking: this is hopeless, we are on a losing wicket. Instead, I was greatly encouraged by what was happening in the country, and excited at the potential. There is the vast area of outreach to tourists and holidaymakers. We never knew who would be in church on Sunday mornings, or what their needs would be. We always had open house for coffee after the service in the vicarage and sometimes some would stay on for lunch. These were good, relaxed times to share Jesus with people away from the rush and pressures of their normal life. We kept the church open every day, with a bookstall, posters, church guides etc being used, and the village folk themselves showing love to the increasing number who visited the church.

Particular events in the church calendar became important times for church growth. Maundy Thursday, when we gathered in the church hall for an informal celebration of the Lord's Supper, was a very precious time. Mothers' Day and the Christingle Service, carol-singing round the fell farms, are just some of the opportunities to preach, teach or witness to the Good News.

But at the end of the day, it is often individuals who are respected in the community who have the greatest influence. An elderly churchwarden with all the gentleness of a true Westmorland farmer, the lady who cleaned the church, the chapel steward who so obviously loved the

Lord, all these and more showed in their daily lives what I was trying to get across from the pulpit on Sundays. During the period of Mission England several vets became Christians and it was thrilling for me as I visited the farms to be met with the comment: 'even the vet talks about God when he visits'.

One cannot overestimate the work of clergy and lay pastors in the rural areas of our country. In Cumbria I was impressed by the dedication of some of the Anglican clergy, men like Colin Reid at Caldbeck, Gordon Scott at Lazonby, and Lawrie Peat on Shap fells. Often under pressure yet patiently loving people into the Kingdom, they are the heroes of today's church. On the chapel side it was the local stewards, doing so much to encourage their often small congregations while reaching out to the young farming lads and lasses, giving generously to bring in evangelists and musical groups.

Keep at it, lads, remember you can't shear a sheep in a hurry and make a good job of it.

Chapter 10

Holy Trinity Church, Aberaeron, Dyfed

Stuart Bell

'Like mushrooms coming up overnight in unexpected places'

When Stuart Bell and his wife first saw the small seaside town of Aberaeron, they fell in love with it, having no idea then that God would later call them to serve the church there, not once, but twice. Stuart is now vicar of Holy Trinity, Aberaeron, where he runs a varied ministry both in the church and the local community. In order to minister effectively in this bilingual parish, Stuart had to learn Welsh and now regularly preaches and takes services in the Welsh language as well as English. The emphasis on house groups is a valuable means of crossing the language divide and pulls members of the church closer together in the body of Christ.

Stuart studied theology in England after two years in industry, then came to Aberaeron as curate. After another six-year ministry in Wales, the Bell family returned to Aberaeron. In addition to his responsibilities for an active parish and a family of three children, Stuart enjoys fishing, caravaning and (like some others in this book) keeping poultry.

'Aberaeron? Where's that then?' This was the question my wife and I were asking some seventeen years ago when we began to sense that the Lord was calling us into the ministry of the Church in Wales. Our knowledge of the Welsh countryside was limited by what appeared to be unpronounceable names, and our understanding of Welsh culture and Welshness was non-existent. At least Aberaeron was easy to say, even if we did not know where it was.

We were trying our very best not to be too romantic about what we felt God was leading us into. We could see that it would be so easy to get carried away by our own enthusiasm and try to imitate some of those exciting stories of dramatic guidance which we had read about in books. How easy it would be to picture ourselves calling the Welsh nation to Christ and being in the vanguard of another great Welsh revival.

However, while I was still in theological college in Bristol, it seemed that the wisest course of action was at least to test that sense of call. We responded to an advert in the *Church Times* and rented a caravan at Nebo, Llannon, and there we had a fortnight's summer holiday. Because Nebo is only five miles away from Aberaeron, we were able to visit the town for the first time, and were delighted with what we saw.

Aberaeron is on the West Wales coast, mid-way between Aberystwyth and Cardigan. With a population of between 1,900 and 2,000, it struggles to call itself a town, as it only has the population of a large village. The town is built around the harbour which has been created out of the estuary of the river Aeron. The main part is Georgian, and tradition says that it was built to a design by Beau Nash. Certainly it is very attractive with wide streets, a central square and well maintained colour-washed houses. As we stood on the harbour wall one sunny day during that holiday, and looked past the yachts and fishing boats which were riding high on a full tide, and saw the church with its tower standing in the centre of the picture we said to one another, 'Wouldn't it be lovely to be a vicar here!'

The next step that autumn was to come to Wales for some parish experience, which was a requirement of the theological college. The only other man from Tyndale Hall in the St. David's diocese was Bill Lewis, who was then the

Rector of Letterston in Pembrokeshire. After three weeks of working alongside him, our call was confirmed in our minds and was tested by an application to the St. David's diocese for acceptance. This was a relatively easy hurdle, but the next was far more difficult. Who would want this young unknown Exeter ordinand who claimed to have a call to the Church in Wales? Who would offer him a curacy?

After months of waiting, from September 1970 until April 1971, and with one unsuccessful application for a first curacy behind us, a letter arrived from Bertie Lewis (now Archdeacon of Cardigan and Rector of Aberystwyth) who was at that time the Vicar of Aberaeron. He invited me for an interview because he had heard about our plans to come to Wales, and at that interview he offered me the opportunity of becoming his colleague.

The church was in many ways on the crest of a wave at that time. The congregations had grown numerically and spiritually under Bertie Lewis' ministry and all aspects of the church's life were in good heart. He had done a great deal of renovation work on the building and also raised the money for and had built a new hall alongside the church. When we think of Holy Trinity as it is today it is with a very deep sense of indebtedness to the clergy of previous generations who have laid such good foundations. The words of Jesus—'I sent you to reap what you have not worked for. Others have done the hard work, and you have reaped the benefits of their labour' (Jn 4:38)—apply very directly to our present church growth.

After being a curate in Aberaeron for three years (1971–1974) we then moved to the parish of Llangeler in the Teifi valley, about fifteen miles away. Then in 1980 Aberaeron became vacant; we were invited to consider returning and to apply for the living. Like many young clergy I had measured myself against most other parishes in the diocese and often asked myself whether I could cope with them. Never had it crossed our minds that we might return to Aberaeron. The very unexpectedness of the opportunity to return was in itself part of the confirmation that this was God's will, because this was not an opening which had been created by human manipulation and scheming. It was with a real sense of destiny that we came back on August 19th 1980 (my birthday). This time we moved into the vicarage, which is a delightful family house, and a new period of ministry began for us.

Building on your Knees

The Rev Basil Gough, principal of Clifton Theological College, used to advise his students to call a prayer meeting as soon as they began a new ministry in their parishes and in that way they would identify the most spiritually alive members of the congregation. The prayer meeting gets bad press these days, but we have felt that the spiritual life of the church must be surrounded with prayer. In order to make sure that this happened we began to meet on a Monday night with the wardens once a fortnight to discuss the work of the church and to pray together. This was the beginnings of a small prayer group which has grown and become to some degree an unofficial standing committee of the PCC. Roy Jones and Gwynne Lewis were the wardens at that time, and with my wife and myself we were a small group of four. Since then we have been joined by Michael Sadler, our curate, and his wife Sally, by David Thomas who is our new churchwarden, and by two new lay readers, David Heal and Peter Tucker.

In many ways this has become a leadership team within the church as we pray together regularly, deal with any immediate problems that arise, and formulate proposals which are eventually presented to the PCC. We don't do it well enough, and we still have a lot to learn about our responsibilities in prayer, but we feel that we have made a beginning, and that no decision that affects the life of the church is made without having been prayed through.

Alongside this we have encouraged the formation of other prayer cells. At the beginning of 1987 we had six groups meeting together, with a seventh in the pipeline which is almost ready to start. These groups have a total attendance of about forty people, which is one third of our committed membership. Each group is completely independent. They decide their own programme, their meeting place, and they sort out their own problems when they arise.

These groups have played a vital pastoral role within the life of the church. A great deal of help and support has been provided for a number of people facing serious personal and family problems.

The formation of prayer groups has had a high priority, firstly because prayer must be at the top of our list of activities if anything of lasting spiritual value is to be achieved. We have seen that we must do more than just pay lip service to the centrality of prayer. We must actually pray. Secondly, it is vital to ensure that members of the church have close spiritual relationships so that they can learn to trust one another, and share their personal problems, and do that independently of the clergy. Those relationships will stand whether the clergy stay or go. Thirdly, it is essential that each group knows the needs of the parish, and so each prayer group leader will be in touch with the vicarage in advance of their meeting to be kept up to date with coming events, and with those who are sick or bereaved. Many people have expressed appreciation that they have been prayed for in these groups. Their ministry is not just for the parish but is nationwide and world-wide. Some of the groups have been keeping their own records of answered prayer, which are very exciting to read. I am sure that what has been achieved in recent years in the church is a direct result of these church members who have faithfully and sacrificially met together to pray.

Numbers Tell a Story

During the last six years our congregation at the main morning service has increased significantly. It has risen from an average of 60 or 70 to an average 120. During the summer season when we are joined by visitors, then we can be 200 to 250—capacity.

One of the lovely things that has happened is that new people coming into the church have noticed and appreciated the friendliness of the church members. They have been struck by the relaxed atmosphere, and the sense of fun which we can share when we are together. Partly this is the result of the fact that we serve such a relatively small community where almost everyone is known by sight if not by name. However, it is also true that the church members are taking seriously the need to be outward-looking as a Christian community within the town.

Another thing that people constantly remark on is the atmosphere of the services. There is often a true sense of God's presence in our midst, and the worship is sometimes quite electric. It isn't always like that, but sometimes we get it right! As a result there has been growth in the size and the spiritual maturity of the congregation.

This growth has come in several ways. There has been some transfer growth because the population of the parish is slowly increasing. Aberaeron has become the fourth largest town of Cardiganshire (now Ceredigion, part of the county of Dyfed) although it is so small. This gives an indication of the thin and scattered nature of the population in our very rural county.

The transfer growth has come about with new families moving into the area both for employment and for retirement. It is to our advantage that the nonconformist churches in the area are all Welsh-speaking, so that any English people who move into the parish have no alternative but to come to us, as two out of our three services on a Sunday are in English. However, we are proud of our Welsh-speaking heritage and have a Welsh service every Sunday which is supported by a very loyal congregation.

The growth through direct conversion to Christ is always the most exciting. Yet interestingly enough there has been no one method which has been more successful than another. Some have made commitment to Christ in the confirmation classes; others during personal conversation in their homes; some during evangelistic events and guest services; others through pastoral visits as a result of sickness or bereavement; some through direct personal evangelism and other through the Sunday service. As we would expect, each person has a different and entirely unique story to tell of the way in which the Lord has worked in his life.

While I was away on a clergy reading party in July 1982, a word of prophecy was given during a time of prayer relating to this parish, and the Lord said that we would see growth 'like mushrooms, coming up overnight in unexpected places'. That prophecy has certainly been fulfilled.

In January 1983 we began to feel that the Lord was speaking to us through Ezekiel's vision (chapter 47) when he sees the river of life flowing from the temple down into the Dead Sea, and bringing life wherever it flowed. It seemed that the Lord was showing us that we were to become a river of life for him, and that we would bring new spiritual life to the parish. This too has been fulfilled, although we are always greedy for more.

Getting it Right

In the spring of 1983 the annual forms of enquiry arrived from the bishop. Usually questions are asked about the size of the Sunday school, attendances at worship, the condition of the buildings and whether the insurances are in order. This year there was the additional question: 'What are your plans for the next four years, and how is your church going to achieve them?'

At our AGM that year it was accepted as a matter of policy that our primary aim for the coming year should be that we pleased God in our worship. Not only that it should be heart-felt, but also that it should be truly united. We wander away from this ideal, sometimes for long periods, but the Lord seems to pick us up again, and to make our worship live.

In order to implement this commitment to getting our worship right we have made some substantial changes to the forms of service we follow on a Sunday. Those changes have been quite painful for some, but at the same time they are important for a growing and developing church. Certain hymns, songs and liturgical forms have become worn out and sometimes lose their meaning altogether. In order to keep our services fresh we are attempting to use the Prayer Book (Church in Wales edition) as flexibly as possible. The framework and skeleton of each service is built around the liturgy but with sufficient freedom to adapt the worship to our needs. As with all change in the church, and in all human society, there is some criticism and dissatisfaction. Some feel that the changes are too ruthless and that the church is losing its Anglican identity. However, because we are now catering for a congregation with a broad denominational background including Methodist, Baptist, Pentecostal, Elim, Brethren, Salvation Army and United Church of Canada (!) as well as Anglican, it is important that to some degree we reflect those spiritual traditions. Anyway, the worship of God is much greater and broader than one narrow liturgical tradition. We have had our own services greatly enriched by those from different Christian denominations who have joined us.

Money Matters

When a man's wallet has been converted we really know that he is the Lord's! Along with numerical growth in the congregation there has also been a significant increase in giving during the last six years. Our budget has gone up from £13,000 in 1980 to £30,000 this year, partly due to inflation, and partly due to increased 'busyness'. We have 'scares' from time to time that we are not going to make the target but so far all has been well. We firmly believe that God will fund the church programme which he has called us to implement.

It is a matter of decided policy where our finance sub-committee is concerned that we tithe our church income. As a result of this our giving as a parish has substantially increased. Last year we gave away £3,000, with our largest donation to the South American Missionary Society which has the greatest support from the parish. One of our church members, Stella Jones, is in training at the moment preparing to go and teach in Chile. We have emphasised tithing as part of the commitment of our church members. We ask that they should give half their tithe to the church (ie $\frac{1}{20}$ of their income). That leaves them with the other half (ie a further $\frac{1}{20}$ of their income) to support Christian work in other ways. Some are now following this practice. We hope that others will learn slowly to do the same.

Growing Mushrooms

Having already had a prophecy for the parish concerning mushrooms, I found myself very impressed with Eddie Gibb's comments about 'mushroom management' in his book *I Believe in Church Growth*. Mushrooms are kept in the dark for long periods and then the door is opened for more manure to be thrown on them from time to time. We are trying to steer away from this style of management where people are kept in the dark about what is happening and are trying to share as many decisions and plans as possible.

Certainly, it is the responsibility of leadership to keep others on their toes, but equally clearly the Holy Spirit has been reminding the world-wide church that leadership is to be shared. We have tried to ensure that there has been a genuine sharing in decision-making through our regular wardens' prayer meetings, and without this loyal and sacrificial support little could have been accomplished in recent years. Alongside this we are trying to encourage a greater shared ministry amongst the church members.

One of the greatest hurdles to overcome and eradicate in a rural setting is the expectation that the vicar will be in everything and always will be taking the lead. It is still just about possible for him to do that in certain circumstances and so the expectation remains. In order to correct these mistaken attitudes, we have recognised certain preaching skills which were being allowed to lie dormant in the congregation, and two men have been licensed as lay readers. Others have been asked to lead house groups and prayer groups, as well as to lead and speak at other meetings and services.

We have learnt three important lessons about shared ministry and shared responsibility. The first is that there is a right and wrong time for this principle to be implemented in a parish. Although it is a clear biblical instruction, we can see that there would have been a time when to implement such a policy in a very stable and settled community could have been destructive rather than constructive. When we began to share the ministry more publicly it was because we felt that the time was right, and the church was ready to accept this advance.

The second observation we can now make is that there is no crisis of manpower in the church. The crisis is of acceptability of the manpower we already possess. There is in the Church of Wales a crisis of the acceptability of the ministry of women (not here, I'm pleased to say, as women participate fully in counselling, prayer group and house group leadership, and speaking opportunities from time to time). However, there is the crisis of the acceptability of the ministry of a newcomer within a settled community. How long does it take to win your spurs and become accepted? There is also the crisis of acceptability of a person from another cultural background and from a different age group. With a significant English immigration into a predominantly Welsh area, there are inevitably tensions. However, this can bring enrichment to the church when each group is showing patience and love towards the other. One instance of that was at a recent prayer meeting where prayers were offered in English, Welsh and French! The gifts are there; the church must simply be brave enough to release them all.

Thirdly, it has come home to us strongly that our church will be unique because of the personalities and gifts of the leaders and the members. There will be no other church exactly like ours anywhere else in the world—because of the unique combination of Christians who belong to Holy

Trinity. This is absolutely right and just as it should be. It expresses the greatness of God, his creativity and his love of variety. He would not want it any other way. As a result of our understanding of this truth, we are not trying to press some kind of straitjacket of church order or leadership or spiritual tradition upon the members, but rather we are try-ing to develop our own individual expression of local church life in obedience to God and using the gifts of the members we already have. This is an important principle to grasp because it doesn't then matter how large or small the community is, and whether or not we have members in the congregation with particular administration gifts or musical gifts or whatever. We can rest content with building a church congregation which is a unique combination of the people who are worshipping together as called by God.

On the Small Side

As the church grows in size so the value of the small house group meeting increases. We have benefited like so many other parishes across the country from the starting of small home meetings. We were advised to take the fortnightly Bible study, which was attended by about a dozen people, out of the church hall. We began to meet in the more in-formal surroundings of the vicarage and the numbers grew. The capacity of our front room, we discovered, was thirty-five—with everyone still breathing at the end of the meeting!

From there we divided into four homes and met for short courses of various kinds. The numbers have increased each time, and we are now about 60 or 70 members in 5 separate groups. Probably the greatest problem is maintaining the spiritual momentum of these groups and ensuring that they are studying material that is of real value. However, there are genuine signs of maturity with initiatives and sugges-tions now coming from the groups themselves rather than just from me. They are developing and changing con-stantly.

One of the great values of these house meetings has been

that friendships have been established in a short period of time which probably would have been impossible through the more formal setting of the Sunday worship. There is an increasing sense of identity with each other, as well as a sense of group loyalty, which has been very beneficial. It is also bringing people together, some who have known each other for years, on a spiritual rather than just a social level. The opportunity is being provided for them to discuss and talk about their faith at a deeper level. It of course also provides an ideal environment for the introduction of newcomers into the mainstream life of the church.

Inside and Outside

Ezekiel's vision of the river of life has constantly been a source of inspiration to us. We felt that God was going to use us to bring new spiritual life to this parish, but we were also praying that he would use us outside the boundaries and confines of Aberaeron. In 1983 we had an invitation to go to the parish of Pentraeth in Anglesey to take a short parish mission there. A small party of three of us took up that invitation. It was followed by another request to help in the parish of St. Peter's Blaina in 1984, and five of us went there. We have since been to Cross Hands in this diocese in 1985, where again our church members had the opportunity to be involved. These invitations have done much for us. It has drawn us more tightly together; we have become more deeply committed to prayer; and we have been strengthened as we have shared our faith and seen the Lord bless what we have said. There are more invitations still in the pipeline, and we feel that we can cope with one or two each year.

Organising the Organisations

Because we are still a very traditional community—like so many rural areas—there are certain aspects of church life which flourish here and yet have died in many other places.

Some say that we are as much as fifteen years behind the times. In many ways that is a great blessing and makes this community still more attractive. Certainly we are able to continue with an afternoon Sunday school which still flourishes because of the dedication of some first-rate teachers. The attendance fluctuates according to the weather as well as the enthusiasm of the children, but we maintain a register of some sixty children and some very valuable spiritual teaching is done through the year.

We also have Explorer and Pathfinder activity nights, as well as a young people's coffee club which is a new experiment in reaching the sixteen plus age group. In a small town these groups provide a valuable social function and are very much appreciated by the parents of the young people involved. One of the great advantages of working with a smaller parish unit is that it is possible to make every single person within the community aware of the church and its work. This was highlighted for us very recently when we had a children's mission, led by June White of Scripture Union. Having visited the junior school and ensured that every child in the 7+ age range had had an invitation, and then following that with a visit to the first year children of the county school, we were able to run a mission where almost every single child of that particular age group within the community (7–12 years) attended at least one of the meetings.

Again because the community is a small one and many of the church people are also deeply involved in other activities in the town, there has to be the maximum co-operation with other organisations both inside and outside the church. It is a deliberate policy on the part of the Mothers' Union to dovetail their own programme into the life of the church, so that there is in no way any competition between the two. As a result many of the meetings complement the other church activities, and some of the programme is arranged to provide extra meetings for the wider church. One event which has been especially appreciated and is now an annual feature of church life is a public debate on some contemporary moral issue. We have dealt with such subjects as Christian involvement in politics, experimentation on the human embryo, women in the ministry and moderation versus teetotalism.

During this current year the MU are sponsoring and arranging a mini-mission as part of their commitment to sharing their faith within the parish. They have invited a guest missioner to come and work with them, and the aim will be to work through small house meetings as well as one or two main evening speaker meetings.

Stable Pulpits

We have a strong commitment to preaching and to teaching the Christian faith from the pulpit! This is the main platform for the instruction of our church members. When a sound re-inforcement system was installed three years ago, we were able to record the sermons, and so have built up our own teaching resource library. We have covered most of the subjects concerned with basic Christian belief and behaviour as well as some Bible exposition series.

However, the pulpit teaching is supplemented by the instruction given through the house groups as well as through other groups which have been drawn together for short courses. Confirmation refresher courses that we have done on a number of occasions have been especially fruitful, as well as enquirers' groups, and a sizeable group has covered the Christian Publicity Organisation *New Life Course*, and the companion *Growth Course*.

Along with the teaching programme we try to encourage our church members to read Christian books. The turnover on the church bookstall has gone up from £180 in 1980 to £1,350 last year, and thirty-five people are now taking Bible reading notes.

Pound of Flesh

It was Matthew Henry who said that for every one time that the devil goes round the parish, he goes seven times around the parsonage. Certainly, he wants his pound of flesh. There has been no ground won which has not been won at a price. The spiritual attacks which we have endured have been severe and very painful at times. There has been a lot of wrestling by some committed praying people:

> Whenever you ripe fields behold
> Waving to God their sheaves of gold
> Be sure some corn of wheat has died
> Some soul has there been crucified
> Someone has wrestled, wept and prayed
> And fought hell's legions undismayed.
> (quoted by Roy Hession in *My Calvary Road*)

It is very difficult while in the middle of some spiritual disruptions or a period of stagnation to be grateful for the testing time. However, it does produce far greater spiritual character amongst the leaders and the congregation. It also demonstrates the fact that the work which is being done is of genuine spiritual value. If it were not, then Satan would hardly be interested in what is happening.

At one period it appeared as though the church was rather like a truck with an open back, and every time the truck lurched forward a few yards then someone fell off the back. It required a lot of time-consuming effort to get that person back on board, and then unfortunately it was only to be followed by someone else falling off. More recently the problem has been a period of spiritual stagnation when the services have been stale and rather uninteresting. Slowly, though, the Lord seems to lead us through these things. There are still tremendous spiritual battles being fought by individuals, and in some of them apparently (hopefully temporarily) the devil appears to win. We cannot by any means claim a period of unhindered and constant spiritual growth.

In order to fight these spiritual battles there have been special times of prayer and fasting. Members have been invited to fast for a day and to spend a half night together in prayer. The spiritual benefit and encouragement from these evenings has been enormous. They have been taking place about twice a year, although they are organised on demand rather than on a particular bi-annual basis.

A Rural End, Not a Dead End

In reading over this report of the church I am thrilled by what God has done for us in recent years. However, it would be easy to give the impression that all is well and that we have no real problems in the church. A brief visit would soon indicate that this is far from true.

No church has ever prayed enough, given enough, worshipped well enough, been pastored adequately nor shown enough love within and without the fellowship. Many problems remain unresolved.

However, the compensations of rural ministry are enormous. The clergyman can know almost everyone in his parish. There is no one who is unimportant. People who normally would never see a vicar from one year's end to the next are visited regularly. The church can play a much more significant role in the life of the community, and can therefore influence it more effectively.

We are pleased that something is happening here in our church, and that it is having an impact on the whole of Aberaeron. Despair, decline and death are not fruits of the Holy Spirit. Hope, growth and life are some of the evidences of his activity. It is our prayer and expectation that God will continue to use us and our church to bring life to the dead spiritual sea which is all around us.

Co-publishers

The Federation for Rural Evangelism aims to enable all those engaged in rural evangelism to benefit from the insights and experiences of others and, together, to promote effective rural evangelism through education and example.

CPAS is a Mission Agency supporting local churches with personnel, training events, and resources.

British Church Growth Association

The British Church Growth Association was formed in September 1981 by a widely representative group of Christians committed to church growth either as researchers, teachers, practitioners or consultants. Following the Lausanne Congress on World Evangelisation in 1974, much interest was aroused in Church Growth thinking, which in turn led to the first UK Church Growth Consultation in 1978. Also during the 1970s a number of denominations had taken some church growth thinking and developed it within their own networks. A number of theological colleges and Bible colleges also began to teach church growth theory, particularly in their missiology departments. The Bible Society had begun to develop church growth courses that were being received enthusiastically. Developments in the work of the Evangelical Alliance led to the setting up of a Church Growth Unit and the publication of a *Church Growth Digest*. This unit drew together a number of leaders involved in the church growth field, but it was agreed to widen its impact by the formation of an association which would be even more comprehensive and effective.

Definition Church Growth investigates the nature, function, structure, health and multiplication of Christian churches as they relate to the effective implementation of Christ's commission to 'Go then to all people everywhere and make them my disciples" (Matt. 28:19). Church Growth seeks to combine the revealed truths of the Bible with related insights from the contemporary social and behavioural sciences. Although not linked to any one school of church growth it owes much to the formulational thinking of Dr Donald McGavran.

Aims The BCGA aims to help and encourage the Church in Britain to move into growth in every dimension. The facilities and resources of the BCGA are available to researchers, consultants, teachers, practitioners and those just setting out in church growth thinking. The Association endeavours to offer practical help as well as encouraging and initiating Church Growth thinking and research.

Activities   The following are among its activities:
1. Producing a quarterly journal particularly geared to the British scene with practical, biblical and theoretical articles of help to the churches as well as offering a forum for the sharing of views. 2. Producing a number of occasional in-depth papers on a variety of topics. 3. Co-publishing books on Church Growth. 4. Running a specialist Church Growth book service offering discounted books to members and producing a catalogue of recommended church growth reading. 5. Operating a reference system for information and personnel. 6. Organising a biennial residential conferences on particular topics of Church Growth relevant to the church in this country eg Church Planting 1983, Conversion 1985, Bridge Building 1987. 7. Encouraging, co-ordinating or organising lectures and seminars on particular subjects or with particular speakers which could be of help to the churches. 8. Carrying out research in allied fields and building up a research register of work already done or being undertaken in various centres. 9. Monitoring church growth at home and overseas. 10. Linking in with a European initiative to share insights peculiar to the continent of Europe. 11. Encouraging grass-roots involvement through seventeen regional groups.

Government   The Council of the BCGA is made up of 15 elected members and 7 co-opted members who meet 3 times a year. Although members serve in a personal capacity, the Council aims to be representative of geographical region, denomination and churchmanship, practitioner, researcher and teacher.

The day-to-day running of the Association is carried out by an officer with some secretarial assistance and the active support of members of the Council. The offices are situated in St Marks Chambers, Kennington Park Road, London SE11 4PW and the telephone number is 01-793 0264. The BCGA is a registered charity, no. 28557.

Membership   Membership of the BCGA is open to both individuals and organisations interested in or involved in the theory or practice of Church Growth. On payment of an annual subscription members are entitled to receive the *Church Growth Digest* (the journal of the Association) four times a year, information about activities through the Newsletters, special discounts on conferences and books, membership of the Church Growth Book Service, voting rights to elect members to the Council every two years, links with other researchers, teachers, practitioners, and consultants on a regional or national level as well as help or advice on allied matters.

The current subscription is £8 for individual membership and £17 for organisations or churches.

Further information about the Association and membership is available from the Secretary, British Church Growth Association, St Mark's Chambers, Kennington Park Road, London SE11 4PW.